The Banality of Heidegger

JEAN-LUC NANCY

The Banality of Heidegger

TRANSLATED BY JEFF FORT

FORDHAM UNIVERSITY PRESS
New York ▪ 2017

This book was originally published in French as Jean-Luc Nancy, *Banalité de Heidegger*, Copyright © Éditions Galilée, 2015.

Fordham University Press has no responsibility for the persistence or accuracy of URLs for external or third-party Internet websites referred to in this publication and does not guarantee that any content on such websites is, or will remain, accurate or appropriate.

Fordham University Press also publishes its books in a variety of electronic formats. Some content that appears in print may not be available in electronic books.

Visit us online at www.fordhampress.com.

Library of Congress Cataloging-in-Publication Data available online at http://catalog.loc.gov.

Printed in the United States of America

19 18 17   5 4 3 2 1

First edition

Contents

Translator's Preface
Both/And: Heidegger's Equivocality

JEFF FORT

The Banality of Heidegger is a text that intervenes in a highly charged and still unfolding situation: the ongoing publication in German of Heidegger's *Schwarze Hefte* or *Black Notebooks* and the response to what they reveal regarding their author's vision of something he calls "world Jewry" (*Weltjudentum*). What they reveal can only be called "anti-Semitism," regardless of how this might otherwise be qualified (as metaphysical, as historial . . .). In addition to the urgency of such an intervention, which belongs to several registers at once— ethical, philosophical, historical—there is a linguistic register, as well. In *The Banality of Heidegger,* Nancy is writing about a set of texts that have only recently been published in their original language (some 1,800 pages so far in the German volumes, with many more to come) and that have therefore only begun to be translated. Nancy's commentary will thus reach many readers before they have been able to read the texts by Heidegger in question.[1] This situation is integrally a part of the commentary itself, if only insofar as it makes it necessary for Nancy both to translate for the first time the passages he cites and, more generally, to paraphrase the contents of the *Notebooks* as these relate to his analyses. This work of translation and paraphrase on Nancy's part (and then of course on my part) should continually be kept in mind, for reasons I would like to specify in what follows. In doing so, I will also lay out a number of specific translation issues that will help orient readers in navigating this multilingual field (French, German, English), particularly in relation to other existing translations of Heidegger or of works on Heidegger. Finally, I would like to put forward a humble plea that readers see this book for what it is, rather than looking to it for what it very clearly is not, but that, one has reason to fear, many might have preferred it to be: it is neither a defense of Heidegger (far from it), nor a wholesale consigning of the philosopher to the dustbin of a cultural and political history that we have supposedly left behind. Instead, it takes the "case of Heidegger" as one dense moment in something much broader and extremely profound—namely, what Nancy indicates as a self-hatred constitutively haunting the West, this "Occident" whose very name evokes its own decline, along with the urge for renewal and foundation that appears to have programmed its self-understanding since long ago.

First, then, the question of paraphrase: aware that many of his readers are likely not to have access to the German texts he is reading, Nancy often elaborates his analysis by condensing and paraphrasing segments of Heidegger's *Notebooks* in ways that an inattentive reader might confuse with Nancy's own statements. The lines between the two are not always heavily drawn, but they are discernible and should always be kept in view. Again, this is worth emphasizing, given the stakes of the discussion as well as the unpalatable nature of some of the material being paraphrased.

Nancy's French in this book is thus closely intertwined with Heidegger's German, all the more so when he translates into French directly from the *Notebooks* (as he does in every case). While I have consulted the German texts that Nancy quotes, and have on some occasions (very few) rendered these quotations more literally with respect to the German or in ways that correspond to established conventions in Heidegger translations, I have by and large remained close to Nancy's French, even when Heidegger's text might point in a different (English) direction. I did this with the sense that this is above all a translation of Nancy's text and that his choices in translating Heidegger are integral to this text and reflect his understanding of Heidegger.[2]

For the sake of clarity, and so as not to interrupt the text with an excessive number of explanatory notes, here are a few points where divergences from existing Heidegger translations should be noted.

Historial, historiality: Nancy himself points out, in reference to one quotation from Heidegger, that his use of the term "historial" corresponds to *weltgeschichtlich*, literally "world-historical"; but "historial" has also been used more generally to translate Heidegger's use of *geschichtlich*, a word that commonly means "historical," but that in Heidegger corresponds to the notion of what is authentically or properly historical and indicating a deeper historicity (*Geschichtlichkeit*) than mere *Historie*—history conceived as a positive discourse, often translated into English as "historiology" (and *historisch* as "historiological"). I have chosen to give Nancy's term in English as "historial" (and "historiality" for the substantive, instead of "historicity" or "historicality"). It is worth pointing out that "historial anti-Semitism" corresponds also to what Peter Trawny has called *seinsgeschichtliche Antisemitismus*, which has been translated literally as "being-historical anti-Semitism" in, for example, Trawny's *Heidegger and the Myth of a Jewish World Conspiracy.*

Beginning: This crucial term translates Nancy's *commencement*, the ordinary French word for "beginning." It corresponds to the German *Anfang.* Because of the emphasis and importance placed on this term and its variants by Heidegger in a number of his texts, many English translators have used "inception" (likewise "inceptive" or "inceptual" for *anfänglich* and inceptuality for *Anfänglichkeit*), or in other cases "commencement"—this in order to mark such terms as a set of interlinked and operative concepts and to distinguish them from the less frequent use by Heidegger of *Beginn*, to which he gives a somewhat different and contrasting sense. Since there is little occasion here for any confusion with the latter term, I have simply used "beginning" (likewise "begin," etc.) based on Nancy's use of the ordinary French word. In two instances (in Sections 9 and 11), Nancy writes *le commençant* for Heidegger's substantive *das Anfängliche* ("the inceptual"), which I render as "that which begins."

Destining: Nancy systematically uses the term *envoi* for Heidegger's *Geschick*, which is often translated into English as "destiny." *Envoi* is related to *envoyer*, to send, and so is a sending or send-off (terms that I find a bit awkward to render *envoi*). While the notion of a destiny or destination is clearly implied, there is for Nancy, I think, a slight tilt in the direction of the initial moment, the beginning point of the "sending," and for that reason I have translated it as "destining." If, on the other hand, this may appear to take some weight off the end, arrival, or fulfillment, the latter is no less operative and should always be kept in mind, as well.

Meaning (sense) of being: The phrase from Heidegger (especially the Heidegger of *Being and Time*) that translators have rendered as "the meaning of being" is *der Sinn des Seins*. This is translated into French as *le sens de l'être*, literally the *sense* of being, and elsewhere Nancy has developed at length this sense of "sense"—or "meaning" (see, for example, *The Sense of the World*). On those occasions when this ambiguity arises, I have tried to keep both of these senses in view. It is worth noting that the "meaning of being" in Heidegger leans in any case rather toward meaning as "sense" and all its connotations than toward meaning as signification (which corresponds more closely to German *Bedeutung* and French *signification*).

In addition to these points of language, I would like to make another broader point, and, as mentioned, to offer a plea that this book be read for what it is and not as failing to do certain things that it explicitly (and, one can argue, justifiably) does not wish to do. I do this not because Nancy's positions or arguments need defending—they are perfectly clear and as such need no extra pleading from me—but because the often polemical discussions around this topic may well merit placing further emphasis on what the book actually means to say and do and on the true scope of what it proposes.

There are two points of view in particular, diametrically positioned, that this book purposely steers between; schematically put, these are: Heidegger's thought is untouched by the faults of its author; and: Heidegger's political, moral, and intellectual compromises render his work worthless.

Between these extremes stands a fact, which Nancy clearly considers to be such, and which serves as a basis for his analysis: the *Black Notebooks* reveal that Heidegger was anti-Semitic, *philosophically*, within important aspects of his thought itself. And Nancy has little patience for equivocation on this point, or for attempts to diminish it by pointing out, for example, that it is in "only a few statements" out of the bulk of the *Notebooks* that this perspective emerges. His response is clear: so what?[3] Indeed, can there be such a thing as a proportionally small amount of anti-Semitism, especially when this supposedly small proportion immediately occupies a world-historical and metaphysical plane? Nancy does not think so. This fact, then, lies at the basis of the book and constitutes the substance of its analytic task.

One can imagine, then, at least two poles in the response to this fact. One would be precisely to attempt to mitigate or even to counter it with arguments that would somehow diminish or safely circumscribe the condemnation that it entails. In the face of Nancy's book and its obvious condemnation, this could lead to an "it goes too far" argument, on the part of those who wish to defend Heidegger's work against the growing taints and tinges that have, over the decades, seeped further and further into its internal folds. One might even think it possible to expect such a defensive argument from Nancy himself, a "Heideggerian" thinker and "disciple" who, in light of these labels, could be imagined to have some interest in defending the beleaguered master. One need only read the title of the book for this caricature to be dissolved into its own lack of substance—this title with its provocative and damning allusion to Hannah Arendt and to Eichmann, which Nancy so clearly and persuasively justifies in the first pages.[4] The text itself leaves no trace of such a notion. What remains, instead, is an analysis driven, in fact, far beyond Heidegger himself (a movement, I would add, unmarked by any Oedipal drama), in order to touch on the deeper grounds of the problem: the place of anti-Semitism within Western thought and "civilization" at large. At this level, and on this scale, Nancy goes only as far as the signs and symptoms take him (to a very radical depth, as it turns out). In this perspective, "defending" Heidegger against the "accusation" of anti-Semitism would be trivial and pointless. The case, as to "whether," is settled. But the forms, consequences, and implications of "how," in what sense, and on what basis, remain of great interest. It is there that Nancy's purpose lies.

They remain of great interest, that is, unless one thinks that the very notion of saying anything substantive about Heidegger, of engaging with his work at all, is itself a sign of dupery, charlatanism, or hypnotic subjection—an intellectual and even moral compromise in its own right. This is the other pole. Stated most schematically, its all too familiar logic goes like this: Heidegger was a Nazi; his philosophy is obfuscation, mystification, and sibylline nonsense; and now we have confirmation that he was an anti-Semite. There is nothing more to say—or to read; or to think about. Heidegger is finished. In the face of this attitude, there is indeed not much one can say. If such a preconvinced reader picks up this book, it will likely give rise to an "it doesn't go far enough" response—whereby, in fact, the only length one need measure would be that of the rope with which Heidegger hung himself. (How else to explain his wish to publish these *Notebooks*?) What I mean is that this "not far enough," which is primarily a demand for vociferous denunciation, is actually one of the most restricted responses possible: either sheer and total condemnation, or nothing. The problem with such a position (one of the problems) lies in this "finished." Is Heidegger, and with him all that his work involves and represents, really behind us? Here, too, Nancy obviously does not think so. And it is disingenuous to think that it is so, even if one did believe that there is nothing of philosophical value to be had from reading Heidegger.

But Nancy does not believe this, either. He affirms here, at least implicitly, that Heidegger remains an important philosophical resource. And that, like it or not, he remains, indeed, one of the most important thinkers of our age. Like it or not, this problematic figure will forever hold a prominent place in the landscape of twentieth-century European philosophy—neither, certainly, as the only legitimate voice in that landscape (as Heidegger himself seemed at times to believe) nor as an unfortunate perversion or a merely clownish sideshow (although even appreciative readers might see aspects of this). The problem, of course, is that he also was, in fact, a former Nazi and, we now know, a thinker who put the clichés of anti-Semitism to work within his thought. This, then, is the simple assumption that Nancy inhabits, uncomfortably, and expects his readers to acknowledge as well: Heidegger is both of these. He was *both* an erstwhile Nazi given to anti-Semitic "thinking" *and* an incisive philosopher whose radical questioning was driven by the urgencies of his epoch. Heidegger is *both* indefensible *and* not simply dismissable. This is the unfortunate knot that Nancy attempts, not to untie, but to show in its most far-reaching intrications.

To defend or to dismiss, then, would both quite gravely miss the point.

Instead, the point would be to continue the analysis—which means also to continue reading—and, in a true work of critique (in its original sense of distinguishing, separating, deciding, judging), to locate the points at which a monumental body of twentieth-century thought articulates itself with the dangers of *its own* thoughtlessness and ruination (and not only those of the epoch it haughtily diagnoses, though of course these are intertwined). Is there a difference between what Heidegger called "the unthought" and a crude and blinding thoughtlessness within his thought? Is there a way to separate Heidegger's thinking from his stupidity? Is there a legitimate and an illegitimate Heidegger? Perhaps not, but now it is no doubt in part by way of such awkward and inadequate questions that Heidegger the genuine philosophical resource will have its chances.[5]

There is, however, a moment in Nancy's text that suggests something perhaps even more troubling and dangerous for Heidegger's chances than the one-sided and polarized positions I have evoked here (between which there is of course room for many varying shades of ambivalence). In a note toward the end of Section 12, in reference to the possible emergence in Heidegger's later texts of a "beginning" that would extricate the event from an inherent "destining," Nancy writes that to explore this possibility, "one would have to consider Heidegger's entire itinerary," and then adds, rather tartly, "assuming one still had any appetite for this. . . ." In a sense this offhanded but withering remark may be the most devastating in the entire book. It evinces, on the part of a thinker for whom a long and complex reading of Heidegger has been deeply constitutive, nothing so dramatic as an anguished repudiation or a "loss of faith" or anything of that sort, but rather a mere loss of . . . taste. Nancy's word here is "*goût*," the taste whose absence easily edges into something stronger, a kind of *dégoût* or disgust. There are certainly moments of disgust in this book, and of overt anger—but one may wonder whether the possibility of such a quiet turning away, on the part of many otherwise deeply interested readers, may have further-reaching consequences for Heidegger's oeuvre than any thundering condemnation.

That being said, one might nonetheless decide, as Nancy appears to have done, that it is precisely the deeply *equivocal* nature of Heidegger, his work, his very mixed legacy, that calls for reading, thinking, analysis, and critique—that there is something singularly critical, indeed, to be gained from such work, and something constitutive of what Nancy calls "our history." That is ultimately where he wants to draw our attention.

And that is where I will leave this preface, in favor of Nancy's own far-reaching propositions. Suffice it to reiterate that the scale and scope of these propositions leave Heidegger far behind—that is, they shrink him to the size of one moment within a broader historical thinking that is, in its own way, world-historical, though in a sense very different from Heidegger's tales of historial destinies. Nancy's turn in these analyses toward the birth and development of Christianity, in its foundationally ambivalent relation to Judaism, and then, within and beyond Christianity, toward a dynamic and destructive self-hatred lodged in the heart of the West, will not be surprising to anyone familiar with his ongoing work carried out under the rubric of *the deconstruction of Christianity*. This thinking, which includes dimensions that are indeed both world-historical and locally narrative, both philosophically synthetic and of necessity empirical, both broadly schematic and incisively critical, provides the taut and cutting thread that takes us from Heidegger's banality into the volatile core of a history whose decisive and unsettling events continue to unfold.

The Banality of Heidegger

The title I give to this study comes very clearly and directly from Hannah Arendt. This should not give rise to the misunderstandings that have occasionally been provoked by the subtitle of her book *Eichmann in Jerusalem*. Indeed, "A Report on the Banality of Evil / *Ein Bericht über die Banalität des Bösen*" has been misunderstood in a way that is surprising if not troubling, as if it were a question of declaring that the evil represented by the Nazi camps was something banal and so did not deserve to be unreservedly opposed and denounced. The expression chosen by Arendt was judged to be a failure both of intelligence and of the heart (with regard to the victims), as well as of analysis (with regard to the Nazis). This interpretation took the "banality" in question as a relative indifference of evil, whereas it was rather an attempt to indicate the contrary: the extent to which it had been possible for the judgments and practices that converged in the extermination of some five million people to be made into a banality.

It may well be that Arendt's judgment regarding Eichmann was skewed by the defense strategy, which we now know was elaborated at great length by the former chief of Section IV-B-4 of the Head Office for Reich Security in the hopes of distracting the court's attention—but this does not invalidate the thought of the "banality of evil." Eichmann was no ordinary functionary, either in terms of his functions (both visible and secret) or in terms of his notoriety. It is nonetheless possible to say that his defense strategy was inspired precisely by the reality of the immense order-execution machine whose functioning was made possible only by a form of normalization and banalization of those orders and their deep motives. Subsequent work by historians and analysts of the phenomena of mass destruction have corroborated Arendt's intuition.

If I recall these givens—themselves banal today—it is because the misunderstanding has nonetheless been tenacious and because it is enough to pronounce the expression "the banality of Heidegger" to see this misunderstanding quickly arise once again. I have been immediately suspected of wanting to minimize the importance of the anti-Semitic statements revealed by the publication of the *Black Notebooks* (as if, for example, I had wanted to recall that the black of these notebooks is nothing more than the color of their covers—which it is—and that any association with a spiritual darkness would be out of place . . .).[1]

But the opposite is the case (as it was for Arendt): we have to do with a phenomenon of much greater scope in time and space, in which the possibility of what Arendt had confronted is contained. The banality, in Heidegger's case, is that of the *doxa* of anti-Semitism as it was circulating in Europe in the years 1920–40 and as it has reemerged in our day, particularly in France and in Germany, in Greece, and a little everywhere.[2]

Among numerous possible confirmations, I choose this passage from an article on the anti-Semitic laws of the French government of Vichy. Considering the commentaries (supposedly "neutral and objective") on these laws offered at the time by legal specialists, Danièle Lochak places them under the sign of banalization and then specifies the following:

> The word "banalization" refers to two convergent processes, to a double effect of enshrinement and euphemization. There is a banalization of anti-Semitic laws in the sense that there is an enshrinement of a new discipline, which takes its place among other disciplines and is integrated into the frameworks and categories of common law. In addition, there is a banalization of anti-Semitism itself through the effect of euphemization, of derealization, produced by the conversion of a logic of anti-Semitism into a juridical logic: perceived through the abstract veil of juridical concepts, the anti-Jewish measures lose all concrete content for commentators and readers; their tragic consequences disappear behind a purely formal treatment of the problems they raise.[3]

With Heidegger's *Black Notebooks*, the "conversion" thus described can be transposed from the juridical to the philosophical register, thus making it possible to speak of the introduction into philosophy of a banality—the very one to which the juridical discourse of Vichy bears witness, as well as that of the anti-Semitic discourse that was very widespread in Europe since the beginning of the twentieth century. This discourse produced almost mechanical effects of adherence on the majority of all those who were not protected by any thought capable of critiquing the historical, anthropological, philosophical, and fantasmatic crudeness abundantly contained in this discourse. Such a capacity for critique could have arisen from democratic or religious, Marxist or humanist convictions. It could also come from a repulsion felt toward the intellectual vulgarity inherent in racism, this vulgarity that Nietzsche had very clearly detected. Heidegger, in his notebooks as well as in the *Beiträge* (*Contributions*) repudiates the racist or racial principle precisely because the first depends on the second, which for its part proceeds from a biological, naturalist, and therefore "metaphysical" conception.[4] To speak of the "animal endowed with reason" is to remain, twice over (race and reason), on the hither side of the necessary "transformation of man into the founder of Da-sein"[5]—that is, of the coming of being [*l'être*], or even *as* being [*être*].

Now it is indeed the putting into play of "being [*être*]" (without an article) as coming, arrival, event (*Geschehen*), and destiny (*Geschick*), irreducible to any substantial or substantifiable given (such as "Being" [*l'être*], precisely) that the initial and essential resource of Heidegger's thought resides.[1] The difference between being and beings constitutes not a difference of terms, but that *différance* without concept in which Derrida transposed the most proper effectiveness of the philosopher in whom he recognized the most determined and most vigilant form of what he called, in 1967, "the reduction of naive ontology."[2]

The reduction of ontology certainly does not lead back to the hateful banality of anti-Semitism. It is even deeply foreign to the latter, and the thought that Derrida developed in relation to Heidegger manifests this with great clarity. We will return to this in the end. For the moment it is a matter of understanding how, at least during a certain time, anti-Semitism—banal and unthinking by definition—could be convoked by the thought that put "being" in question.

This putting in question, which we are more familiar with under the name of *Destruktion/deconstruction*, demands another ontology, and something other than an ontology, however "fundamental" the latter may be. Heidegger states that the "second beginning" begins "neither as theory of knowledge nor as 'fundamental ontology'" but as "metaphysics—in an essentially new sense."[3] Which also means that it must always recall within itself (*erinnern*) the *phusis* of the first beginning, even if this one, the second, begins with *alētheia*.

Now it is exactly with respect to this new beginning (a second or "other" beginning as Heidegger most often qualifies it) that the unfolding of the West, in its present state of "uprootedness," is rigorously improper. It is improper with respect to a new beginning because this unfolding knows only calculation and explanation (*Erklärung*, a casting of light, not far removed from *Aufklärung*, enlightenment).[4] With calculation one can "do nothing" or "undertake nothing"—which in German is *nichts anfangen*, literally "begin nothing."

It is a question therefore of being able to (re)begin. The situation that does not cease to occupy the *Überlegungen* (reflections) of the years 1938 to 1941 is that of the impossibility of finding access to another beginning,[5] except on condition of a complete disappearance of what characterizes the West in its ultimate condition: technical knowledge, the domination of the masses, calculation, and "machination."[6] For Heidegger, the present situation offers no other possibility than the annihilation toward which, in any case, the set of determinations and forces engaged in modern machination are tending, and this includes the war—in its third year in 1941 and beginning to become doubtful as a war on several fronts.[7] The hypothesis that these problems could be settled on a global scale—"planetarism"—does not reach to the level of the history of being, or of the "historial," for it is only a version of "the order of the masses."[8]

At this point, toward the end of the year 1941,[9] a distinct motif appears, one that had already been generally evident in the preceding notebooks but that is here considerably reinforced and whose presence we are familiar with after the war, as attested by the lecture of 1945 on "Poverty."[10] This is the motif of "Russianness" (*Russentum*) as an element that, in its truth or in its authentic properness (*eigentlich*),[11] remains separate from the European-Western determination. To the extent that technics and communism confront the European West, machination is engaged "in a formidable self-annihilation of its own forces and tendencies." With this self-annihilation (*Selbstvernichtung*) one glimpses, as a very faint suggestion, not the possibility properly speaking of the new beginning but at least that of a sort of counter-type (by the rebirth of completed metaphysics) whose occurrence can contribute to letting another beginning begin.

There can be no question here of lingering on this consideration of a Russian authenticity as a reverse side of communism (intrinsically linked to technics, Heidegger has previously recalled). The point is rather to emphasize the importance of the characterization of a spiritual properness grasped in the nomination/configuration of a people. Likewise, without developing an analysis of the role played by the idea of a "people" in these notebooks, as elsewhere, one can note the following: a people—which is not a race—can be considered as a spiritual force (although Heidegger is wary of this vocabulary), or else more precisely as a force of historical beginning. This force must arise from an appropriate encounter between a humanity and a divinity (this latter understood not as creator of man but as a sign addressed).[12] A people is what arises from this encounter/response and what thereby opens a historial possibility.

> It is not "by" him [the god] as his "creator" but by a decision toward him in the correspondence of essence between divinity and proper humanity that from the human essence comes a people who supports the founding activity of the essence of truth.[13]

The Russian people, today (1941), is not yet such a people, but it represents no less the character or the only outline of a character capable of indicating a possibility for a new beginning—one that perhaps still awaits a German people. The latter, however, would have to be removed from what is in the end the "machinating" condition to which the Nazi regime has led it, itself betraying what it had seemed capable of opening up as a beginning. As for the other peoples—English, French, Italian, American, Japanese—it suffices to indicate here that they have been characterized at greater or lesser length in their insufficiencies or in their deep miseries. We must no doubt specify that it is not always exactly a question of peoples (it is more a question of "Americanism" than of the American people) and that in any case entities like Christianity, on the one hand, and technics, on the other, form characters that are transversal to the peoples they affect in an essential manner and that constitute the West—*Abendland*, the region of the evening and of decline.

We have thus brought together the necessary conditions for situating anti-Semitism. The exigency of another beginning brings with it that of a people capable of assuring it—just as the first beginning was the doing of the Greeks. The fulfillment of the complete destruction of the Greek beginning also brings with it its appropriate people.

3

This appropriate people is the Jewish people. Heidegger states this very explicitly in terms that fit within his overall position with regard to the problem constituted by the West—that is, with regard to the destiny or the historiality of the West.

> The question concerning the role of *world Jewry* is not a racial question but the metaphysical question that bears on the type of human modality which, being *absolutely unbound*, can undertake as a historial "task" the uprooting of all beings from being.[1]

"Historial" here translates *weltgeschichtlich* [literally, "world-historical"]. This expression as used by Heidegger provides the entire justification for Peter Trawny's adoption of the term "historial anti-Semitism." Much in the manner of "the banality of evil," this expression immediately raised suspicions and protests on the grounds that it would minimize Heidegger's anti-Semitism by projecting it into a rarefied sphere of speculation that would exempt it from all participation, direct or indirect, in the Nazi enterprise of extermination. Once again, this is a misconstrual that betrays a desire for vehement accusation and scathing denunciation at the very point where a reflective analysis might well increase the gravity of the case by considering it in its full scope and import.

It is in fact remarkable that the same use of the word "historial," accompanied by the word "spiritual" as a way to characterize the deep truth of anti-Semitism and of the extermination, provoked no protest at all when Philippe Lacoue-Labarthe had recourse to it in 1987 and later.[2] This reveals a sort of conditioned reflex that has appeared more recently: words such as "evil" or "anti-Semitism" must not have associated with them terms that are not overtly charged with condemnation. . . . To condemn is one thing, to analyze is another, which in any case cannot damage the condemnation, any more than it can favor it. The obligation that we face today belongs above all to analysis, not because we ought to forget moral judgment (or political or philosophical judgment), but because up to now we have still not gone far enough in *thinking the deep reasons for our condemnations*. Two-thirds of a century after the extermination we have not yet sufficiently confronted what has happened *to us*, to European humanity become fully global in the time and in the movement of events that Heidegger designated as "the uprooting of every being" after, at the same time as, and still before a hundred other expressions seek to name them and to interpret these events ("decline of the West," "reification," "alienation," "*Kulturpessimismus*," "obsolescence of the human," "catastrophe of modernity," "homogeneous world," "one-dimensional man," among others).

What is at stake in the reading of Heidegger, and specifically of the texts most exposed to condemnation or anathema, is that they place us once again, but with a very particular force, before the exigency of interrogating that which, with "the modern world," happened to the world—and to the world as such—that is, as a presumed configuration of one or several possibilities of making, of receiving, and of dividing up and sharing sense (whatever one may understand with this word). Now it was Heidegger who operated the first metamorphosis of the philosophical question of sense (or meaning: *Sinn*) by designating it as the question of "the meaning of being."

It is undeniable that he did this at the same time as others—Bataille, Benjamin, Freud, Wittgenstein, to name only these—but that his operation was the most frontal in that (if one can speak thus) it directly tackled ontology, the architectonic theme of "metaphysics" that Kant, Schelling, Hegel, Nietzsche, Kierkegaard, Bergson, and Husserl had set out to place in question or in crisis. There is something a little ridiculous in having to make such a reminder, but it does seem necessary, given the widespread opinion that Heidegger could without further ado be struck from the ranks of the philosophers on the grounds of his Nazism. This amounts to piling one serious error on top of another: first, that the event of Nazism, of all the fascisms, and more broadly of the totalitarianisms *and* of democracy (which pretends that none of this applies to it), would not pose any philosophical problems (except as a vague call to "values"), and then that Heidegger was simply a Nazi (like Bäumler, let's say)—whereas in fact the *Black Notebooks* demonstrate exactly the inverse. Let us cite one sentence from volume 95, which brings together all of the philosopher's contempt for Nazism: "Racial knowledge, pre-historical knowledge, knowledge of the people constitute the 'scientific' foundation of the populo-political world view."[3]

That his manner of posing the question would lead him not toward Nazism as a "world view" (an expression that he rejects for philosophical reasons), but toward something that one can characterize as an "archi-fascism," to use a term from Lacoue-Labarthe, or else as a kind of hyperbolic revelation of a destinal truth of being based on "a people" (I use the word "revelation" here with the intention of specifying it later)—this is what deserves to be scrutinized more closely, dismantled, and repudiated. But that this gesture was a philosophical one is something that cannot be denied.

This only renders more acute the questions with which we are unambiguously confronted by the *Notebooks*.

4

It is evident first of all that "historial anti-Semitism" is a characterization that is entirely justified. It gives in abridged form what the sentence quoted above begins minimally to develop: the Jewish people, as such, plays a determining or even primordial role in the "uprooting of being." Given over entirely to itself—"totally unbound," "unattached," or "freed"—this people proves to be very singularly appropriate to, and given to, the task of uprooting. It is the privileged actor in the decline of the West, or at least it presents the most characteristic figure—the "type," the sort, the mode— of such an agent.

A first question arises: why is it necessary that a movement so broad as the one embodied all at once in Americanism, Bolshevism, democracy, technics, rationality, and objectality would have recourse to such a singular figure—since it cannot be doubted that not all the actors of this catastrophic history are Jewish?

Certainly this necessity corresponds to the very principle according to which a people is necessary to set to work every decisive disposition of history-destiny: this disposition is not simply a process, it is a commitment, a decision taken and taken again in the form of determinate figures and by the bearers of these figures. This necessity here takes a turn that is at once very precise and very singular: the Jewish people claims for itself a racial principle. Such a principle itself comes from a "domination of life by machination."[1] But the machination that gives rise to such a naturalist principle leads in the direction of a complete "deracialization" (*Entrassung*) of a humanity reduced to the undifferentiated equality of all, and in general of all beings.

It is interesting to note that the argument is not very far removed from the one in which Marx qualifies money as a "general equivalent" in which productive humanity is alienated and flattened down from its own proper existence and therefore from its value or meaning [*sens*]. This parallelism in the perception of a leveling and a nondifferentiation is almost duplicated by another parallelism of a very different nature: that between a class destined to overturn class relations and a people destined to annul the distinction between races. What is the most common in the two perspectives is the recourse to a determinate and privileged instantiation—a privilege that in each case is made prominent by its negativity: the proletariat and the Jewish people are both excluded from humanity. They are both endowed with an identity that is entirely negative and/or negating. What this parallelism suggests, though I do not claim to offer a deeper analysis of it, is a certain eschatological and figural regime of thought: an end is approaching—an end, and therefore a beginning—and this advent requires a figure, the identification of the annihilating force. (One cannot even stop at the fact that the proletariat inaugurates a revolution, whereas the Jewish people engage an involution, since, for Heidegger—we will come back to this—the shipwreck is indispensible to the "new beginning.")

There must be, therefore, a new type of humanity, of "modality of human existence," through which is accomplished the downfall of a humanity not only "all too human" but above all too estranged (alienated?) from its proper destination: as Dasein man is called to put being at stake, or to offer the opening by which being [*l'être*] is placed at stake—that is, is exposed to *being* [être] (as a verb, not a substantive) as the meaning, the sense, of its own putting-at-stake, where meaning (sense) also *is* this putting-at-stake.

There must be, therefore, this very singular dialectic of an identity of the upheaval of identities that are located and consolidated by the substantive (thing-like, objectal) interpretation. This identity must be more or less than "humanity": more when a "people" has its "provenance" in the "essence of the human" (and therefore overcomes this essence), and less when another "people" (but in fact why not the same? one is pushed to ask) turns out to be a type committed to an uprooting from being.

"With deracialization there occurs a self-alienation [*Selbstentfremdung*] of people in an indistinct unity [*in eins*]— the loss of history—that is, of spaces of decision regarding beyng."[2] The proper, nonalienated site of humanity insofar as it is able to overcome itself is none other than history, therefore the advent of the events insofar as they can make it possible to decide (oneself) with respect to "being"—which "is" not but which destines itself as the possibility of destining itself with/by/for its non-beingness [*non-étance*] (if it is possible thus to condense this thought).

It is therefore necessary that a figure be given, a type of humanity deciding to forget "being," the no-thingness [*néantité*] of what metaphysics has taken for a supreme or general being. This entire construction depends perhaps on this: there must not and therefore cannot be either supremacy or generality. No supremacy (or sovereignty) because each existence opens the stakes of "being" in its entirety (*jemein*, as *Sein und Zeit* also says),[3] no generality for the same reason: the "proper" (*eigen*) must be properly "itself." The insistence on the existent insists also on ipseity.

From this there follows a sort of implicit rule of exception: no generality can contain or offer the exception that must be constituted by the opening of a true possibility of "being" or of letting being "be." Every singular beginning requires a people. As does every ending.[4]

5

And it is very much a question of ending. The West is bringing itself to an end, must bring itself to an end, or else is
precipitated into its ending. Is being "essentially" condemned
to oblivion and to a complete lack of heirs to receive it, or do
forgetting and devastation come to it from elsewhere? But
then, from where? They somehow come to it both from
within (*beyng* is effaced or crossed out constitutively, one
could say) and from outside (ontology arrives, it comes, even
if it is already "in" the origin). This arriving or "coming about
[*survenir*]" that also "comes" from or within the "beginning"
itself is inherent to it insofar as there is "beginning" and
therefore becoming. Coming-about belongs to becoming
[*devenir*]. At the same time, becoming is understood as
"destining"—which goes toward the effacement proper to
that which begins. But to what extent in these conditions is
there any "coming about," properly speaking? And if there
is, does this then leave becoming without any surprises?

The question remains in principle extremely difficult, and I cannot claim to examine it here. But in these notebooks it receives a de facto response: the Jewish people—this people considered at least as a remarkable exception at the heart of all the forces of destruction that it accompanies and of which it seems also to provide the type. The Jewish people is the identifiable agent, properly identifiable (or *more properly*, a bizarre notion that must no doubt be recognized), of what at the same time is a broad composition of masses and identities, American or Americanism, communism and technics, French, English, Europeans, Germans even, and "*Abendland*," evening, decline, collapse.

At bottom, the "decline of the West" is a pleonasm. The West, the "Occident," is decline in its name, in its topological determination—a place turned toward the setting sun—and in its destiny, in its *envoi* or initial sending, and in this destining of "being" that it is or that it forms—that is, of a decision. For Heidegger, the West bears within itself a fatality (*Verhängnis*, a recurrent word in the *Notebooks*) that belongs in a constitutive way to the destiny and to the destination of being. One can read in *Überwindung der Metaphysik* ["Overcoming Metaphysics"] (a text from the years 1936 to 1946) the very particular insistence of his thought on the necessary character of the unfolding of metaphysics—that is, of the domination of beings arriving at the devastation of the world and thus gradually bringing "after a long time the sudden irruption of the beginning."[1]

It is not my purpose here to investigate this necessity of a decline inscribed in the first beginning and indispensable to the coming about of the other beginning. This is obviously a very important and very broad question in Heidegger's thought during this period. It is even, in more than one respect, the guiding motif and the most active driving force of this thought. In the framework of the present study, it suffices to state that the anti-Semitic motif is inscribed very clearly at the heart of this configuration: the Jewish people belongs in an essential way to the process of the devastation of the world. It is the most identifiable agent of this devastation in that it presents a figure, a form or a type, a Gestalt— the figure of the aptitude for calculation, of traffic, and of shrewdness.[2] But this figure is precisely "one of the most hidden and perhaps the oldest of the figures of the gigantic."[3]

The figure of the Jew configures the very type of a devastating necessity: the gigantic, calculation, and a rationality that is busy de-differentiating the world and properly dislodging it: withdrawing from it every kind of ground and soil. *Bodenlosigkeit*—groundlessness, lack of soil—is a distinctive trait of "Jewry." Groundlessness consists of—or leads to—"being bound to nothing, making everything serviceable for itself (Jewry)."[4] Thus no real "victory of history over the historyless" can come about until "groundlessness excludes itself" (*sich selbst ausschliesst*—one can note the euphemistic character of the term, which however can only designate a destruction, an elimination).

How is it that *das Judentum* can suppress itself? We may wonder whether this kind of wish is a reprise of what Kant had designated as a "euthanasia" of Judaism, which would have led the way to the true moral religion.[5] And in a certain way, it is possible to think that it is: Judaism must or should suppress itself since it is at once in error and in truth. What for Kant was understood in terms of the progress of human consciousness becomes in Heidegger a self-suppression of what is worldless (of the gigantic, of indifference), making possible the other beginning. What is thus proposed is nothing other than the West's long feverish wait for its own reconciliation: its own nonpainful identification with itself.

The Jew will have been the name and the index of a failure to identify itself, to recognize itself, and to accept itself.

But how it is that the *Bodenlos* can come to exclude itself—this is what remains enigmatic. How can exclusion strike the exception that in and of itself has already designated itself as excluded?[6] Here again a question arises that exceeds the limits of the present study—but that must eventually receive a response. In other words: how can the destruction of the world and of history—of the possibility of a meaning of *beyng*—be destroyed by itself or of itself? Why and how is it that at the height of devastation "there continues to shine [and is therefore undestroyed] the light of a history capable of decision"?[7] This question is in any case manifestly correlated with the question already raised: how does the first beginning engage its own devastation?

At the very least it is necessary, according to Heidegger, to admit that the first beginning harbored in itself—in itself, at its edges, despite itself . . . —the force and the figure of its forgetting and then of its destruction. While one may well understand that the unconcealment of "being" bore within itself its own forgetting, it remains all the more obscure why this forgetting would have required a continuous, centuries-long, and univocal devastation; even more obscure is the necessity to produce or to adopt a singular figure, identified and perfectly visible, of the devastation as such.

6

For Heidegger—who in this regard only confirms a *topos* dating at least from the Renaissance—the first beginning is Greek. The fortune (*Glück*) of the Greeks is to have "dared to determine themselves from out of being."[1] It is in this sense that the Greeks were a people, the people of the beginning. It is remarkable that this Greek singularity appears in isolation, without being in any way related to a historical environment. The history that then opens presents itself on the contrary, and from the outset, if not as cosmopolitan, then at least as the mixture and the vulgarity of which Rome will provide the first figure ("despotism of opinion and mishmash"),[2] and all that followed will constitute its continual aggravation. The beginning is brought about by a people (in the strong sense of the word), and the decline is brought about by the mixing, confusion, and indistinction of peoples in a humanity that does not place high enough the *humanitas* of man, as the "Letter on Humanism" will affirm.[3]

Conversely, however, the precipitation of the decline that precedes and announces the coming of the other beginning is signaled by a figure—a people? Perhaps, but at the same time the reverse side or indeed the caricature of a people—who concentrates in itself the traits and the dispositions of the decline.

That the forgetting of being (that is, not of *das Sein* but of *Seyn*, noun, verb, and cipher of the event and of a saying [*Sagen*] according to which the destining of all beings unfolds) can only bring in its train the forgetting and lack of heirs of the people of the beginning—this is something that might be admitted insofar as it is indeed necessary that this take place somewhere, in some language; but it would remain to be known how, in the midst of what, and in relation to what, this people abruptly arose (a question concerning the "before" of philosophy). On the other hand, it is less easy to understand how the decline would be provided with a figure-people of forgetting and of a "mishmash" of peoples.

From where does Heidegger draw this figure? Quite simply from the most banal, vulgar, trivial, and nasty discourse that had long been scattered throughout Europe and that had been propped up for some thirty years by the miserable publication *The Protocols of the Elders of Zion*.[4] The proximity of his statements with this text (the themes of calculation, of democracy, of manipulation, of internationalism) can leave no doubt. This proximity does not require that we attempt to ascertain whether Heidegger did or did not read this crude and grotesque fraud of a document. Its existence was simply the effect and the reflection of widespread opinions, which found more and more pervasive acceptance as

Europe had ever more reasons to feel itself caught in the "discontents" that Freud had named in 1930.[5] As early as 1921 the *Protocols* were revealed as a fabrication: in the world of culture and the university, it was possible to have knowledge of this. To remain close to its claims, without citing the text but also without demarcating oneself from it, could not in 1940 be the result of chance.

Heidegger knows very well what he is doing. He is collecting banal rubbish for the sake of higher ends. Which means also that he recognizes a higher truth in anti-Semitism. A truth so much higher that it cannot even be published without being associated with the critiques of Nazism and of Christianity (which are different, to be sure, but also interlinked) that fill the text of the *Überlegungen*. These latter therefore remain private and are held back from publication until far into the future. This higher truth is the one whose scheme I just outlined. This scheme merits the support of the most widespread, heinous, and narrow-minded vulgarity because this vulgarity says in its way the truth of Jewish-being, of *Judentum*, the perfectly identifiable entity and identity of the precipitation of the world into vulgarity, precisely and in every sense of the word.[6]

One could say that Heidegger shares the banality of a public mentality [*esprit*] for which the Jews embody a devouring banalization of the world—the loss of the spirit of peoples in the universal-vulgar (*all-gemein*, as he sometimes writes).[7]

One can ask: did the configuration of thought go in search of the anti-Semitic motif, or was it, conversely, the anti-Semitism that suggested a part of the configuration? It is difficult, no doubt impossible, to decide this question. For Heidegger, anti-Semitism is not only ambient, for this ambience also bears within itself an entire vein of thought that in certain respects is already traditional: the thought of the people, that of a history whose moments and flexions belong to peoples themselves defined as singular or even as exceptional subjects. There occurred in the first quarter of the twentieth century a conjunction between the themes of decline, of the masses, of democracy and the many forms of a will to be startled or shaken up, to regenerate and to eliminate the morbid factors of the West. Heidegger ties together the deconstruction (*Abbau*) of metaphysical ontology—a grand philosophical gesture that extends and pushes further the premises of Nietzsche, Kierkegaard, and Husserl—and the destruction (*Zerstörung*) of that which and of those who seem to him precisely to be destroying the world and history. Thus, in connection with the interpretation of Hölderlin, which demands that "positive history (*Historie*) first be surmounted," what is required is "the destruction of the absence of historiality [or of destinal sending, *Geschichtslosigkeit*]."[8] But this absence of historiality is a distinctive trait of *Judentum*, which moreover is characterized by the lack of everything that allows for the opening to *beyng* (soil, destiny, decision, people). It is therefore a matter of deconstructing metaphysics and of destroying the forces that bring to full completion its deleterious work [*oeuvre*]. It is necessary to destroy destruction[9]—which is already itself a quite singular destruction of self (of the spirit of beginning).

The logic and the economy of this deconstruction/destruction of destruction propose a quite singular interweaving of self-affirmation and self-destruction. The West destroys itself, thus fulfilling a necessity of its destining, and it requires the destruction of its destructiveness, so as to liberate another beginning that, while other, must for all that be no less truly or authentically *its own*. And what if it were a question here of a self-rejection constituted at the heart of the West?

It is around this motif—at once intuited and yet never brought out as such—that thought and anti-Semitism come to be bound together in a knot that is, however, untenable.

7

Heidegger could have investigated for himself the reasons and the provenance of anti-Semitism. But he didn't. He received as a given of the Western destiny the banality that henceforth became the gravely hateful and ponderously grotesque discourse of the *Protocols*. This thinker who was so adept at tracing provenances, whether those of the Greek language or those of modern (technical, democratic, calculating) devastation, did not ask himself where anti-Semitism could have come from. It is a given, as we saw; it is one "of the oldest figures" . . . (and if this "figure" is not biological, it has nonetheless, in the absence of any other analysis, a sort of "natural" aspect about it).

There were, however—there are still—grounds for asking oneself how it happens that the very broad modern consensus—Americano-Bolshevik, techno-democratic, and in particular Anglo-Franco-European—includes within itself, as a remarkable figure and a leading agent, this Jewish element on which all the others have been so eager for so long to cast their opprobrium. In and of itself, this circumstance deserved more attention from someone who painted the picture of devastation with such broad strokes. Not only is this devastation a self-destruction, but this self-destruction corresponds to the aptitudes and to the designs of an entity/identity that at once belongs to the entire history of the West *and* forms in its midst a detestable exception. This exception has two aspects: *Judentum* is an exception since it brings the destruction of the West—in this sense it is the exception of the hatred of self—but it is also indeed, *within* the hatred of self, the exception of a foreign intrusion. Perhaps self-hatred necessarily includes an intrusion and a tearing apart of and/or within proper intimacy. It would still be necessary to be able to presuppose this proper intimacy, for example, as "Greek" (as it is necessary to presuppose a "subject" in order to think any relation whatever with a "self"). Here too lies open an interrogation for which I can indicate no more than a starting point.

Why does Heidegger not engage in any way in an analysis either of the hatred of self or of the hatred of the Jews? Did he know the book by Theodor Lessing that appeared in 1930, *Der jüdischer Selbsthass* ("Jewish self-hatred")—a work whose turbulent reception caused something of a stir? Was it not possible to learn from this book that Jewish self-hatred (anti-Semitism internalized by Jews—one relevant example here being Husserl)[1] translates the depths to which this hatred can reach: the very depth of identity or of being-a-self, for it is exactly to such a point that anti-Semitic repulsion wants to reach. The whole of Europe (of the West), posited in its self-affirmation (*Selbstbehauptung*, a word that for Heidegger serves alternately to denounce complacent Western smugness or to celebrate the decisive affirmation that looks toward the beginning), repudiates at its heart a foreign body that threatens it precisely because it disperses, dissolves, or conceals its "self." Dispersion, dissolution, or concealment of self—it is ultimately to these that Jewish specificity is reduced.

With or without Theodor Lessing, Heidegger was perfectly able to enter into a reflection of this order. Did he not write, "mindfulness of self [*Selbstbesinnung*—one could also translate: meditation in, on, and of self] proper to the emerging age of the transition from the first beginning to the other beginning has a singular character—for here the self-conquest [*Selbst-gewinnung*] that is to be prepared must be strong enough to abandon what is usual and has been granted up to now."[2] Such a formula is after all only banal in a context—itself banal, as banal as anti-Semitism—of spiritual renovation. But it takes on a particular relief if one asks what or who this "self" is or can be, of which or of whom one must boldly know how to abandon all that is received and habitual, for it amounts to the same: either the new "self" must be entirely original, or it must be the fruit of its own metamorphosis with renunciation, sacrifice, and reformation.

But everything that must be renounced (as shown by what follows in the text) is of course nothing other than that of which the Jews are the agents or the embodiment. Up to what point then will it be necessary to reject, repudiate, or sacrifice the Jews? It will inevitably be necessary at least to reject them as "Jews"—that is, to take on the Jew "in himself" (the calculator par excellence). The Jew in himself in both senses of the expression: the one who recognizes himself in *Judentum* and the one inevitably carried in himself by any Western person who is not yet in a state of opening himself to the new beginning. In any case, it will be necessary to sacrifice him,[3] or it will be necessary that he "himself exclude himself," as we have already seen, which ultimately means perhaps that every form of suppression of the Jews and every form of suppression or auto-suppression of the West (of the devastation) amounts to a renunciation of what is "received and ordinary" in the long error and/or wandering of the West.[4] (But is it not the conversion of the Jews that the relatively more restrained forms of anti-Semitism—Kant's, for example—has always demanded, and does not a conversion imply the renunciation of an "old man"?[5] The theme of the "new man" is in any case closely bound up with that of [re]beginning.)

The fate that must be hoped for or sought for the Jew, who is groundless and has no soil, no history, no people, and no identity other than destructive calculation, can in any case only be one or another form of exclusion, of casting out. The destining of *beyng* toward a new beginning of its *Geschehen*—that is, the destining to its renewed and retrieved destining, overcoming itself by destroying the destruction that its forgetting has engaged (its own forgetting, the forgetting of itself that it opened with itself)—this destining demands the ending of what in any case foments the scheming of the end: the West, the metaphysics of beings, the historyless, the groundless, and the peopleless. To have done, therefore, and above all, with this people of the peopleless, this entity/identity that plays against and with the Nazis the fallacious game of race, that is, of nature,[6] whereas it must be a question of *beyng* alone.

The mobilization of anti-Semitism takes on all its meaning and its truly "historial" dimensions from the moment when it is clear that the Jew is the oldest figure of a self-destruction of the West, a self-destruction that is its truth as advent and destiny of the forgetting of *beyng*. This forgetting itself belongs to the "self-positing" of man who posits and reposits himself on himself,[7] thus making himself executor of the scheming that itself proceeds from the intrication of the metaphysics of beings in the first beginning. This intrication is also that of the singular figure of the Jew in the midst of the West, which for its part is given over entirely to the manipulations of this figure that at the same time it rejects (without for all that knowing the true reasons for this rejection, which only now takes on its historial dimensions).

8

And yet, this rejection is there, since long ago, albeit in the ignorance of its own historial truth. But Heidegger gives no attention to the long provenance of anti-Semitism. He does not question (any more than does the most banal *doxa*) the fact that it comes about with Christianity and in sum at the heart of the birth of Christianity, of which diasporic rabbinical Judaism is the "twin brother."[1]

Why this lack of interest or at least of questioning? Why not seek to situate the appearance of *Judentum* in the history of the West? To be sure, Heidegger never burdens himself with the questions of a historian, no more when it comes to the transition from Athens to Rome than for those from the Mediterranean to Europe, from the Middle Ages to the Renaissance. Everything seems to fall within a single and continuous process in which what comes about are only the successive aggravations of the metaphysics of beings. At most one can find considerations on the properly modern regime of science and technics, as if the industrial and then the cybernetic age alone represented a truly important change, although always guided by the same erosion of the meaning of *beyng*. (This erosion began with Plato, as the "Reflections" often recall. And yet Plato is not Jewish. The Jew came along to intensify and unleash Platonism.)

Why? One can give two schematic responses.

The first consists in saying that the considerable—not to say exclusive—philosophical weight of the motif (concept? Idea? drive?) of the beginning ultimately prevents consideration of any development, any history in the simplest sense of a succession of events. In that regard, Heidegger would have been the first to designate in a philosophical manner the decidedly untenable character of the progressive models that had governed the thought of history from Kant to Marx. Without dwelling on something that would require an investigation of its own, I will limit myself to the following assertion: namely, that the domination of the beginning, as it engages the development of the ebbing and extinction of the force of the initial to the point where it lets another beginning surge forth (regarding which one does not know whether in turn it will or will not place in danger its force of inauguration; in what way will it be "other" while also being "second"?)—this *archeotropy*, then, which can no doubt be seen throughout the history of the philosophies, of the arts, of religions, and of specific forms of knowledge in the West, might constitute the symmetrical danger of a *teleotropy* that has marked our culture at least since the middle of the eighteenth century. Of course one understands, and indeed must welcome, the rupture that Heidegger introduced in relation to history.[2] It cannot be deduced from this that the archeotropy should not be analyzed as a mode of annulment of history—that is, precisely of the *Geschehen* of *Geschichtlichkeit*: of the historical character—happening, taking place, coming about—of historiality itself. Tendentiously, Heidegger annuls this *Geschehen* himself. . . .

The second response consists in turning toward history, precisely, toward a history that is perhaps not historial or otherwise "arriving" and "destining," and therein to analyze the event of anti-Semitism. To remain very succinct, one must say: this event is bound up with the birth of Christianity, which is itself bound up with an internal transformation of the Judaism of Israel. The Judeo-Christian gemellity of the first centuries of the common era can be regarded, for many reasons that cannot be laid out here, as a mutation in the identity of the West and of Westerners: the mutation of a relation-to-self that was like nothing before.[3] Between these twins is played out—one is tempted to say: of course—a rivalry, an agonistics, and also a hostility. Judaism transforms and transports with it an identity already received in a form belonging to the earlier world (kingdom, territory, and temple) and that, in one very complex movement, emerges in two forms (to simplify) that in turn give the two twins. Christianity detaches itself from the received identity (the one called "Jewish people"). But it gives itself its proper identity only in a universal dimension according to which it must (1) reject Jewish identity and (2) fabricate for itself its own substitutes for the identity it will therefore never have received. Marcionism testifies to this desire to found the self on itself,[4] and the entire construction of the "heresies," as well as the canon of "Scripture," bear witness to the same desire. Thus, when Christendom confounds heaven and earth, Caesar and God, the pope and the emperor, it sees itself confronted with a Judaism that, for its part, does not confound, and whose silent reproach becomes hateful to it.[5]

Anti-Semitism appears early in the history of Christianity. It develops there by emphasizing each time that Christendom reworks, in a complex and risky way, its own identity (in the crusades, in scholasticism, in the Reform—to mention only these). Christendom becomes Europe, European humanism, and its mastery of nature and of history. Its identity is thereby transformed and is also always troubled once again: with industry, democracy, and the modern state, Europe does not know what it is becoming. What it experiences as disquiet, or even as a danger, it places upon the Jew—whom it has already condemned to be groundless and without history, to wander and to handle impure money (which the Christian handles, too, but under the legitimacy of the church). One ends up with the *Protocols of the Elders of Zion*, while at the same time provoking the birth of a "Zionism," another Judaism that itself divides the Jews—a development in which Heidegger is not the least bit interested.

In order to discern the motives and driving forces behind the Christian rejection of the Jews—as a restricted configuration of a difficulty of being a self, or even of the West's self-hatred[6]—we must examine Christianity. To examine it, it is necessary to distinguish within it what attaches it to Judaism and what detaches it. Heidegger at times uses the epithet "Judeo-Christian": he does not for all that interrogate this conjunction, which, however, is traversed also by a disjunction that is violently anti-Semitic (or "anti-Judaic," if you like, but this was never at bottom anything but what unfolded as anti-Semitism). He does not question it despite the fact that he himself quite often elaborates a distinction between two Christianities. The one deserving of every criticism is frequently accompanied by the adjective "apologetic" or is explicitly related to the church and/or to its dogma. This distinction remains silent, in fact, regarding what might be neither "apologetic" nor ecclesiastical and dogmatic: there subsists a sort of suspense, a hollow space.

Let us take only one example: when Heidegger critiques the "ambiguity [*Zweideutigkeit*]" of a Christianity that by turns plays up "the affirmation of the world and the hope of the beyond,"[7] he seems not to suspect, on the one hand, that there is possible in Christianity itself an entirely different understanding of this double postulation and that, on the other hand, Judaism does not lend itself to this ambiguity, or not at all in the same way, and finally that the gemellity of the two is situated no doubt precisely in this vicinity.

Had he attempted to explore it more deeply, Heidegger would no doubt have discerned how "non-apologetic" Christianity (let's say—to give a simple reference point—that of Angelus Silesius or else of Kierkegaard and of Augustine, as they are evoked at one point)[8] can be indebted to Judaism for something that cannot be simply reduced to the Western scheming of reason and calculation. And yet because he proceeds silently or furtively to such a distinction, and because he is unconcerned with the flagrant discord that divides the "Judeo-Christian" accord (which he sometimes calls "Christo-Jewish,")[9] Heidegger allows a glimpse in his own work of the possibility of an attention that immediately represses the historial zeal.[10]

If this attention had been able or had wanted to be exercised, it could have placed in evidence the extent to which "apologetic" Christianity (dogmatic, ecclesial, dominating the two kingdoms) had to do with a fierce desire to constitute itself as the alpha and omega of a history henceforth recognized as a "history of Salvation" and consequently to affirm itself and found itself as the *Verus Israel*. If there must be a true Israel, then every other one is false and everything that bears a sign of Israel must be intrinsically false.

Thus it becomes possible to associate the Jew with a curse and a misfortune (his own and the one he inflicts) that is pursued and aggravated in a history more and more wrought with uncertainty and disquiet about itself (about its "progress"). It is necessary to affirm a history ordered according to Salvation—even if this history passes through a damnation of the world. To be sure, this is not the schema of Heidegger's thought, but his thought of *Geschick/Geschichte* carried away in Western destruction is not without analogy—and is able to find support, even at the price of a miserable banality, in the denunciation of an agent defined by destruction.

This amounts to confirming that nothing essential has happened in the destiny of the West—nothing except the aggravation of metaphysics and its technical and democratic becoming. Put another way, anti-Semitism is necessary to avoid speaking of anything at all as another *Geschehen* that would have happened or that would have been outlined here or there in the history of Europe. What becomes then of the privilege later granted to Angelus Silesius? To say nothing of Augustine, who, however, will be invoked in "The Anaximander Fragment," and to say nothing of several other possibilities, no doubt, to grasp or to grasp again—in philosophy, in literature, and in art—some signs or signals of *Geschehnisse* not entirely inscribed in the grand final destination that prepares the other beginning?

In other terms one could say: would one not have already and otherwise—erratically—at times rebegun (in) history? Would there not have been more than one history? More and more or something other than "*a* history"? Might not *the historial* be plural, scattered here and there along a path less ordered than the one that this thought assigns to the West? A *destinerrance*, to use a word from Derrida, who in reading Heidegger was perhaps sensitive to an *irren* that, however, appears in the *Notebooks* above all as a way of leaving behind "all correctness and incorrectness" so that "the truth of *beyng*" can "found itself"?[11]

And is it not possible that this perspective does not alter what was opened as a "Destruktion" of ontology? Even better: would it not be necessary to ask whether Heidegger after

1945—keeping in mind that there are still more *Black Note-books* remaining to be read—and especially during all the years that followed, might not have opened some paths in this direction? After all, the grand historial motif, along with that of the "beginning," seems indeed to be complicated, transformed, or blurred in what follows in the work itself. Here again, I can only point toward a perspective for a future elaboration.

9

This would not change the fact that remains: Heidegger's thought, to the extent that it is ordered, in the years 1930–40, around the motif of the beginning and of the historial[1]—of a unique historial—had recourse to anti-Semitism (albeit in a way that is shamefaced, poorly articulated, and concealed; but concealment and confusion are often inherent to anti-Semitism) because this thought remained profoundly riveted to the self-detestation that has never ceased to characterize the West—since Rome at least. We do not like the Jews, or technics, or money, or commerce, or rationality—at least we never fail to distance ourselves from them. We do not like ourselves, perhaps precisely because we would like to be "ourselves"—which most often we believed we had to interpret as "to be Greek," misrecognizing in this way that with and after the Greeks a great deal has happened that did not always come from the Greeks.

But we have needed this image of the Greeks because we do not know how and are not able—or only with great difficulty—to go back any further. But a self, a "oneself," is something that begins, that is supposed to begin itself—produce itself, originate itself, and determine itself—from itself. Heidegger's *beyng* could be described as that which exceeds being-a-self or being as self. But the Heidegger of these *Notebooks* has led it astray into a kind of Self that is the enemy of every other.

Why did he conceal this anti-Semitism in his public texts? No doubt for fear of the Nazis whose anti-Semitism he was at the same time challenging and confirming even while coupling it with anti-Nazism (no less clear although less banal, obviously, and a little less heinous, but only a little, or heinous in a different register). But no doubt also out of a more or less clear sense of the extreme fragility of these "theses" with nothing holding them together except the exalted vindication of an absolute anti-subject Subject. Unless we come to believe that he imagined that later one would be obliged to recognize to what extent he was right. . . . Or unless we think, on the contrary, that since he wanted the *Notebooks* to be published, he felt himself obligated not to continue the concealment, in the end.

Why did he remain silent, later, on the extermination of the Jews, even when he was faced with the friendly but pressing questions of Jaspers,[2] and certainly of several others? No doubt because he refused to renounce the grand schema of *Geschichte* even if henceforth he treated it in a different way.[3] Which means also that to the end he would have (will have?) considered the extermination camps as inscribed in the "destination." A few elliptical declarations on the inhumanity and horror of the camps[4] change nothing in the following two evident facts: (1) for him, the horror of the camps is the extreme destinal point of technics—a proposition that does deserve to be taken into account and reworked, but that however does not imply that (2) there is no need even to mention *who* the victims of the camps are . . . whereas precisely, for him, technics, machination, and the Jews are intimately linked.

He writes, "Das grosse Verhängnis, das überall das neuzeitliche Menschentum und seine Geschichte bedroht, ist dies, dass ihm ein Untergang versagt bleibt, da nur das Anfängliche untergehen kann"[5] (The great fatality that from every side threatens modern humanity and its history is that a decline is refused to it, for only that which begins can decline). A surprising sentence, if the "refusal" of the decline is itself, after all, only an aggravated decline?

But against what can a "decline" be measured if not the presupposition (ideal, fantastical?) of an initial event? And if this initial event harbors in its own destining also the event of its forgetting and of its devastation—that is, if it can only first of all lose its initiality—according to the law of the initial in general[6]—then there is no reason that another beginning would go against this rule. Unless the proper difference of this other beginning had to be precisely . . . not to begin, to displace, and to transform the value of the "initial."

That Heidegger picked up and exploited the banality of anti-Semitism means that he left a place—and not the least important—for a decisive element of the metaphysics of beings: the presupposition of the initial, of the foundation and the origin, of the authentic and the proper. The heinous stupidity, incapable of giving the slightest "thinking" justification to the anti-Semitic motif but quick to draw the portrait of the Devastator in person, was there, available as it was for all the Christian-Roman-nationalist, identitary, and proprietary "selves," desperate to affirm, or even to consecrate a "being-self" whose hideous caricature it was, and still is, expedient to regurgitate onto the scapegoat called "Jew."

To dissociate the "question of being" or of "the ontological difference" from the configuration of originarity or of principality, such is the task, identical to that of dissolving this obsession with the "self," this self-haunting.

Yet Heidegger knew that the appropriative event of a "founding of the truth of beyng" is unique, not in the sense of a unique occurrence but in the sense that each time it is unique and is appropriative only according to the "each time" of this uniqueness.[7] He specifies that this uniqueness exceeds all "eternity" figured as a duration and as a consolation. One can discern in these lines, with the critique of Christianity (let's call it "theological" Christianity), the affirmation of a sense of eternity that owes more to Nietzsche and to Rimbaud, also to Kierkegaard—that is, to a sense of coming into presence *hic et nunc*—than to the projection of an inauguration in the establishment of a new time for which it would be necessary to sacrifice our own. But here "Nietzsche" and "Rimbaud" are names—there would be others—for what has already, before Heidegger, begun to carry away Judaism, Christianity, Hellenism, and our entire tradition outside of itself.

Either a history contains only its own principle, whatever it may be, and this principle destines it to be reduced to a fulfillment—that is, to an absence of history—or else coming-about [*la survenue*] is the principle of every principle, the an-archy of a *destinerrance*, to use Derrida's word. As Elisabeth Rigal has written, "Heidegger's error is to have believed in a *unique* destining"; she specifies that "the idea of an errancy appears very early on in Heidegger" but that "it is always announced from within the horizon of gathering." He will therefore reject the idea of a finitude of sense, arguing that "errancy must not be thought on the basis of destination, but rather destination on the basis of errancy."[8]

It would thus be a question of thinking that if the destining is not unique, then another one, another beginning would also not have the character of a repeat of the unique based on the annihilation of its first brilliance. But it may have already been destined by multiple brilliances, disseminated, more or less recognized—exactly in the way that for Heidegger "each thinker who in the history of Western thought founded a fundamental position is irrefutable; and this means that the rage for refutation is the first waste product of thought properly speaking."[9]

Likewise there is no intention here of refuting Heidegger. Quite to the contrary: by designating clearly the way in which he let himself be carried away and stupefied in the worst of heinous banalities, to the point of the intolerable, one can shed more light on what he himself should have seen and what in any case he allows us to discern.

Heidegger was able to know what kind of trap is contained within the rage for the initial or for the *archi-*. He ought to have known it. His thought implied it. But in the violence of the paradigm of the initial, the old hatred of self, the old rancor of the West against itself persisted in occluding this knowledge.

10

To speak of "rancor" is perhaps more correct than speaking of "hatred" according to the familiar configuration of "self-hatred" to which at the same time we are very close. In French, rancor (*rancoeur*) designates the most bitter and most raging feeling of being the victim of an injustice or a false promise, being tricked, deceived, or rejected. Perhaps the entire West was from its origins infected with rancor against itself precisely to the extent that it promised itself, and still now has never ceased to promise itself, a completion and fulfillment—of nature, of man, of the polity, of justice, of knowledge. Given that Western metaphysics was founded on "the determination of man as present at hand (presencing) animality and vitality," it isn't surprising that it would find its completion in "the predatory animal and the wild beast."[1] Like Freud ten years earlier, Heidegger describes a civilization endowed with an unheard-of violence that places it in a position to destroy itself. Where Freud was deeply troubled and saw no recourse, Heidegger simultaneously dreads and wishes for this destruction. He wishes for it because it is the only means for making possible another beginning, but he dreads it because nothing guarantees the passage to the beginning, or even the definitive completion of the destruction (that is, the self-destruction of the West). Nothing can be properly awaited. At most one can point to a future several centuries away: "In 2300 at the earliest there might be History again."[2] And all that it is possible to say of this uncertain term of fulfillment is that one will then arrive at "a desert commensurate with the emptiness, spreading around itself the semblance of a plenitude that has in fact never been there."

The West will not have ceased betraying itself, essentially, and this betrayal is at the same time the condition for another beginning. Such is the complexity of the "forgetting of being" insofar as this forgetting is inherent to the first destining of being, and moreover without anything allowing us to specify either the reason for this inherence or the reason for its disappearance in the event of a new destining.

There is no question here of engaging in an analysis of this formidable intrication, which makes up the mainspring of the very thought of being as event of its own proper destining. What the *Notebooks* give to consider offers much less the appearance of a questioning that would bear on the exact constitution of the first beginning than, instead, the aspect of a renewed torment.

A questioning on the nature of the first beginning, on its "Greek" character and perhaps even its "initiality" will emerge in the work of Heidegger's later years. Any study of this questioning would certainly be delicate, but it is possible to think that the Western-destinal schema was by then slightly displaced (if we consider, in particular, the reflections on the essential "withdrawal" of being in *The Principle of*

Reason). But in 1937–41, it is a question of relentlessly affirming the necessity of once again "founding the truth of being on the basis of being itself."[3] This affirmation brings with it that always repeated and indefinitely characterized observation concerning the inevitable destruction and obstruction of all History—of every destinal impetus—by the weight of metaphysics (to which precisely the metaphysical, not to say the ultra-metaphysical, constitution of world Jewry contributes). This observation gives the affirmation over to torment, or even despair.

Heidegger writes, "the beginning of the Other is obscure—yet remains that which will produce an essential event [*Ereignis*]: that the Other of another beginning and its distress [*Not*] will be experienced [*erfahren*]."[4] Nothing more, then, than an obscurity in which is outlined the experience and the ordeal of an alterity that must be assumed to be extreme (the other beginning lets the Other begin—which I choose to render with a capital letter, since Heidegger makes it into a substantive) and which at the same time can be experienced only in its needful necessity, if one can thus render the entire value of *Not*: misery in its distress.

One does not know whether to place the stress on this misery or on the absoluteness of alterity. Both of these are to come, to begin, but the beginning can only be of one in the other—and that is its obscurity. In many ways, seventy-five years and so many wars and catastrophes later, we cannot fail to recognize ourselves in this distress. It is indeed the persistence and aggravation of this distress that, for more than half a century, has accompanied the increasing deterioration of the progressive and technicist humanisms at which the notes in the *Notebooks* continually take aim.

Likewise, therefore, we cannot avoid recognizing that, starting before 1940, it was indeed from Heidegger that the impetus and efforts proceeded that would eventually open paths other than those of the progressive humanisms—that of Sartre, in part, that of Levinas, of Foucault, of Derrida, of Lacan, of Lyotard,[5] and even in certain respects that of Deleuze. In their several ways, all of them turned toward various motifs or figures of alterity or of multiplicity. Without any doubt, the themes of "the Other" and "the multiple" must be treated with a circumspection analogous to that required for "the beginning." But it is indeed on the basis of a thinking of an "other" than "being"—a thinking of this other, for example, that Heidegger names *beyng* or else leads back to the *verb* "being"—that the paths will be cleared for a consideration of history that would fall outside the representation of a progressive (or progressivist) fulfillment of beings in totality.

Not only did none of these bodies of thought pick up anything remotely resembling anti-Semitism from the always murmuring gutters of banality, but in various ways a motif of Jewish alterity was introduced—or else was brought to light—in the tradition that had supposed itself to be Greek. By a paradoxical turn that is not without piquancy or (especially) bitterness, it was by way of Heidegger, although despite him—as well as thanks to a number of his contemporaries such as Cohen, Buber, Benjamin, and Rosenzweig— that this motif took on importance.

Despite him, yes, since the obsession with the beginning— with the foundation, with the origin, this "metaphysical" obsession par excellence—led him into the worst and most atrocious of the vulgarities of a hatred of self—of the other-in-the-self—by which is recognized the dreary will to be or to make "oneself." And yet Heidegger was not without some sense of a completely different way, less a way of "thinking" than of bearing or of conduct. A way that turns away from founding-destroying rage and from rancor. He notes, as though in an echo of the analytic of being-toward-death,

"The impossible is the highest possibility of man: grace or fatality."[6] A few lines earlier he evokes grace in relation to the Greek *charis*. He could not be unaware that this Greek work translated—from the Septuagint to the Gospels—the Hebrew noun (*chen*) for a thought that is indeed the one to which we refer when we use the word "grace" in our modern language: the unjustifiable justification that can come from the wholly-outside, in particular when faced with catastrophe, as when *Noah found grace in the eyes of YHWH*.[7]

11

But to find grace, if it is something that one can "find" or encounter in one way or another, one must not seek it or ask for it. There must be some flaw, breach, or insecurity through which it can pass. One can in no way foresee it, or will it, or ever know whether it has even taken place or not. Nor even whether there is any sense in speaking of grace as of something that could be designated, named, circumscribed. Heidegger very much questioned, very much deferred the possibility of what he never ceased calling a task. He held himself until the end in an interrogative suspense, uncertain in appearance but in truth always very certain of what he had named "being"—with the best reasons in the world but without avoiding the risk that by dint of maintaining the invocation of this "being [*être*]" that is unassimilable to the (substantive) "being [*l'être*]" (this *Seyn* or *beyng* under erasure, this being that is no being and is not), he might reinforce the substance of what he had sought to dissipate down to its most minimal semantic element.

This self-assurance made possible the chance that opened up an ineluctable resource of thought, as well as the miserable precipitation into the most sordid sacrificial violence. And we must indeed speak of sacrifice, since Heidegger often speaks of it in the *Notebooks*. It would be necessary to reconstitute in a precise manner the intersecting logics of a warlike sacrifice understood in the most classic manner (which already guided the pages of *Sein und Zeit* on the battle for the community of the people) and of another sacrifice, more elevated, which is the one demanded by *beyng* insofar as it requires the "use" of beings (in the sense of *brauchen* commented upon later in "The Anaximander Fragment" in 1946). I will limit myself to citing one passage:

> What if, in the domain of man, in order to assure the success of one being among beings it is necessary that sacrifices like those in a war be accomplished, which are demanded from man by the appropriation [*Ereignung*] of a word of beyng.[1]

As we see, this is not even a question, it is an exclamation: what is demanded by being is a sacrifice incommensurate with any blood sacrifice—which means not that it excludes this but that it includes it and carries it to an incomparable height. This can be the sacrifice of a people, as other passages show. If we relate this back to the passage already cited in which is found the wished-for destruction of the groundlessness that is proper to *Jewry*, one can imagine without difficulty that the destruction of the Jews by themselves arrives as the collapse of the groundless from the effects of its simultaneous combat against its counterpart (the Nazi racial principle) and against itself (since Bolshevik Jewry fights against capitalist Jewry, and so forth).

One arrives at this: that the destruction of the Jewish people as such could only be desirable *and* would moreover be in one way or another (directly or indirectly "self-destructive") the inevitable program of self-destruction of the West. For it is indeed through the self-suppression of the groundless that the victory "of History over the historyless" can arrive, as the same passage says. It is at this price alone that one can understand the stubborn silence of Heidegger on the camps—a silence that only prolonged the one he had always observed since *Kristallnacht* in 1938 (to mention one significant reference).[2]

As I write these lines—in June 2015—the later volumes of the *Notebooks* have not yet been published, but a few excerpts have been divulged.[3] They show that Heidegger wanted to consider all of Germany as a "concentration camp," because it had handed its fate over to the sorry "world view" of the Nazis, whose racism and technical calculating machination remained deeply foreign to the meaning of *beyng* and of its other beginning.

It was therefore necessary that the agent of Western destruction destroy itself. It is to this that the historico-destinal logic leads according to which *beyng* was destined in its first beginning toward the advent of another, the true (re)beginning in which it will be given to *beyng* to make use of beings and no longer to be covered over by them.

One is left speechless.

The incommensurability of the thinking of *beyng* with any kind of metaphysics of beings gives comfort to the mind of the philosopher before the horror that has never yet been so exposed: he does not turn away from this horror, he wants to extend it to the supposed spectacle of the integral ruin of the West—and first of all of the German people who should have mindfully gathered the meaning of being as wholly-other to beings. In the midst of this spectacle, the technical and calculated destruction of the people who more than any other bore the meaning of calculating domination expresses the truth of the ruination. Heidegger was not only anti-Semitic: he attempted to think to its final extremity a deep historico-destinal necessity of anti-Semitism.

That is why, in the end, the displacement of "biological" racism into a metaphysics of the races perhaps does not displace much at all. Derrida perceived this when he asked, aiming at Heidegger's "equivocal strategy" in some of his texts on Nietzsche, "Is a metaphysics of race more or less serious than a naturalism or a biologism of race?"[4]

It is more serious, without any doubt. As evidence one can cite several passages, such as this one:

> All those, and they are numerous, who now speak "on" race and on belonging to the soil [on *Bodenständigkeit*, autochthony] show . . . that they "have" nothing of all that, to say nothing of the fact that fundamentally they *are* neither of a race nor of a soil.[5]

There is therefore a truth of *being* that is strictly opposed to the discourse "on" race. Race, and with it soil, are linked here with a sense of being and not a manipulation of categories. As he had written of *Mitsein*—of being-with—it must be an existential and not a categorial question. Nazi racism remains categorial—that is, in the end, objectal, operative, and calculating. This is certainly a claim that in many respects can be granted. But the existential thought of raced-being is no less "existentially" (and/or "metaphysically") racist.

The difference depends only on the gap between determinations that are biological—that is, dependent on a supposed science of nature—and a thinking access to the truth of what he later says is indeed "one necessary condition . . . of historial *Dasein*."[6] This access, as could easily be shown in the texts, demands that one find again the true sense and ground of what would be not an objectivized nature, but a *phusis*—that is (to say no more than this here), the form of unfolding proper to *beyng*.

But one remains speechless at yet another level. How must it be understood that the first beginning would have brought with it both the destining of being *and* the ravages of its "forgetting"?

I will not claim here to untangle this very strange philosophical intrication. It may be possible to have a glimpse of this by referring, for example, to certain texts from the years 1938–40.[7] There one can read that the first beginning opened the history of being because it made appear the essence of the history of being, up to then "primordially concealed."[8] Once this history-destiny is unveiled, and even if human beings can believe at moments that they are making this history, it is the truth of *beyng* that is effectuated—that is, that asserts its character as a beginning always rebegun, or rather always rebeginning, and at bottom whose true character is precisely "that which begins" in it, an always relaunched initiality. Perhaps it would even be possible to extrapolate from these texts a motif of beginning that would not begin in the sense of having a continuation, a succession, of consequences (*beyng*, Heidegger also specifies, is neither temporal, nor atemporal, nor perpetual, nor eternal, nor from-time-to-time).

But if this thought does indeed emerge[9]—and although, in the end, one would like for it to have been able to completely extricate the event (as *Geschehen*) from history-destiny (as *Geschichte*)—it clung no less fiercely to a vision that was just as "historical" (*Historisch*) as destinal: the West has passed through a series of episodes across which the veiling of what was initially unveiled has only intensified. Thus have we learned that the unveiling is always initial, but also that it was necessary that the veiling come along to show this to us. . . .

The veiling and obscuring therefore needed its agent, which itself is suddenly and at bottom mysteriously revealed: a people, a race that is "metaphysical" or that figures metaphysics as a darkening destined to better signal the urgency and imminence of clarity.

Everything, then, will have happened—and it is quite difficult not to recognize this—as if Heidegger had absorbed the lesson of a very ancient history: the true beginning is at pains to be marked out as such, for it does not unfold itself according to its truth. It is affected or it itself affects itself with a failure to truly begin—that is, to prime and to found at the same time, in a way that would perpetuate the law of its pure initiality without going astray or breaking down.

The motif of the beginning gathers together all the values of authenticity, originarity, and properness around which is organized what one can rightly designate as a major banality of the most widespread metaphysician's *doxa*. If the first beginning cannot truly begin, this is because it must still make heard its own call, which is made possible only by renewing itself: not by reproducing itself but by manifesting itself other than simply "first," other as definitive, other as event of an advent. The other beginning places human beings in "the necessity of safeguarding the simplicity of the essence of all things"[1]: it does not command a new succession; it metamorphoses succession into a kind of blooming or hatching or into appropriative-coming-about.

It is inevitable to find oneself thus led back into the complex ensemble of Western history, the supposed Greek beginning, and the role of Christianity in this history. For if there is indeed a decisive feature of the Christian event, it is the will to constitute a new beginning—so new that its entire first sequence oscillates between the motif of a rebeginning and that of an *other* beginning.[2] Now this oscillation is constitutive of Christianity in a somewhat recurrent manner. I have already evoked this and will bring together now what I take to be essential, for what concerns us here, in this formula: Heidegger attempted to think another beginning that would be simultaneously in the image and in the place of the other beginning that Christianity wanted to constitute (through one of its aspects, at least: that of the church and "apologetics").

It was important to him, therefore, above all not to retain the traces of other beginnings throughout the history of the West, and especially not at the points of its most perceptible inflections (Christianity, the Renaissance, the industrial and democratic revolution). At the same time, the rejection or the exclusion of the Jews by Christians aims to reject and exclude something that could complicate or even disturb the strict Christian initiality. Let us therefore keep this in view, even if we do not stop to examine its nature or its stakes and to conjoin it with the rejection of Christianity itself.

Furthermore, in the history of Europe the rejection and the exclusion of the Jews have continually played the role of a displaced denunciation of something in the unfolding of "the" civilization that turned out to be, like it or not, not very Christian at all—not very "elevated" or "spiritual" and even frankly "base," material, and "grasping." It is not necessary to insist on this point: in a very continuous and sustained fashion, anti-Judaism and/or anti-Semitism have been maintained, renewed, and aggravated according to the changing rhythms and forms of the need for justifications (that is, of the disquietudes and anxieties) of modern, capitalist, technical, entrepreneurial, and controlled society. That is where the banality lies: in the very long persistence and increase of this rejection, which is nothing other than the rejection of a supposed bad or false principle (or beginning) embodied or rather endured in a people, a race, a figure designated and destined (messianic, therefore, or in some way Christic).

To limit ourselves to one example, there is nothing surprising in affirming that Heidegger repeats in his manner these sentences from Marx: "Christianity originated in Judaism. It has now been dissolved back into Judaism" (that is, based on the context, "self-interest, practical need, egoism").[3]

The banality of evil is above all the fact that a motif of rejection and of purgation—therefore and conjointly a motif of regeneration, of rebeginning, or of metamorphosis—comes to fly like a tattered ideological rag presented to every gaze and to "the strange conviction that a fundamental change of hearts must follow the downfall of any given human institutions"[4]—which is a way of characterizing one possible mode of the revolutionary conviction. Now it is indeed a question of revolution for a Heidegger who (for example) stigmatizes "machinations" that are only "apparently revolutionary."[5] The National-Socialist revolution falls short of being truly revolutionary because it does not rise to the level of the other beginning.

This banality corresponds to a "mass" society equipped with ever greater means of communicating and diffusing messages capable of provoking indignation and condemnation, along with the expectation of a prompt advent of forgotten authenticity. Heidegger was able to read the banners in the streets of his city bearing these words: "*Judentum=Verbrechertum*" (Jewry or Jewishness=criminality or criminal association). He retranscribed their substance into his notes, as many others did, in public or private notes, during these same times.

Not only does this banality not lessen any of the gravity here, it rather weighs everything down all the more. It weighs on thought in one of its essential points. How was it possible that a thinking that felt so intensely the heaviness of a morbid state of civilization could, in the face of the anguish, find nothing but to add to this anguish the imprecations forged by an age-old false or bad conscience? This question is not only aimed at Heidegger: it addresses itself to us, to all of us, to every exercise of thought, today no less than before.

It is not enough to condemn the ignominy of anti-Semitism: we must bring its roots into the light of day—and this means nothing less than intervening at the very heart of our culture.

It is not enough to condemn the extreme violence with which we immolate peoples, as well as social categories, classes, or strata: we must ask ourselves what obscure sacrificial resource operates thus, and in view of what "sacred" entirely devoid of sacrality (of symbolicity, if you prefer).

It is not enough to look with stupefaction upon a history that appears to us to race toward its own ruin: we must learn to break with the model that this history has given itself: that of progress in a conquest of the world by man, and of man by his own exponential finalities.

It is not enough, finally, to understand that *being* submits itself to no "ontology": we must still yet withdraw it also from the nomination of a *beyng*, as well as from every other nomination, and from the destination that every name no doubt draws along in its train.

In other words, we must learn to exist without being and without destination, to claim to begin or rebegin nothing—and also not to conclude.

Coda

Between the writing of this book and its publication, many things have been written, said, and peddled about concerning Heidegger's *Notebooks*. Many attempts have been made to separate from their author the infamy attached to anti-Semitism. These attempts succeed above all in showing to what extent they must rely on interpretive ruses, denegation, blindness, and a refusal to read. These efforts thus contribute to reinforcing the necessary denunciation.

For all that, no one seems to worry about what is at stake insofar as Heidegger's thought cannot simply be struck from our history. The Nazi enterprise that this thought wanted to exceed by reducing it to a crude domination, so as to bring its impetus to the heights and vigor of a "new beginning," did not suddenly arise from nothing, and neither did this thought. Rather, it was born from an exigency felt throughout the culture of the West. What happened to thought happened to us, happened to our civilization and through it. In this sense, Heidegger's "Reflections" also represent a terrible lucidity with regard to what he considers to be worse than the fall itself, "since there is lacking the essential *height* from which one could fall."[1] How many are there among us—we old Occidentals—who do not say the same thing today?

We are henceforth in charge not only of the destructive and self-destructive horror, but also of everything that indulges in beginnings and ends, in Orients as well as in Occidents, in sunrises no less than bloody sunsets.

If this has happened to us, and if it happened [*arrivé*] precisely with the thought of arrival—of *Ereignis*—it is in part because this thought itself did not manage to pull itself away from the desire for foundation, for inauguration, and for schematic programming. What Heidegger discerned as the metaphysics of beings, as the choice of that which *is* within the releasement of that which is not but that arrives and drifts, he nonetheless held onto the motif of rebeginning—that is, of an initial and self-sufficient form of what is—or even of what must be. In other words, he held onto the logical, political, veritative, and destinal auto-foundation: the very thing, then, that the most constant modern thought, be it Heideggerian or otherwise (or even very hostile to Heidegger), is often very far from having abandoned, whether it believes itself to be logicist or subversive, revolutionary or reactionary.

In anti-Semitism there is hatred of something that withdraws itself from auto-foundation. This hatred is repeated in anti-Christianism (so abundant in the *Black Notebooks*) while also taking up from the Christian doctrine the pretention to a proper foundation that rejects its Jewish provenance—its provenance in errancy and wandering.

Most assuredly, being is not. But history is not confined to being the destiny of its forgetting. It has no doubt also, and since long ago, escaped from this destiny, or else it has made it wander, has made it err, and still does.

Supplement

Volume 97 of the *Gesamtausgabe* (*Anmerkungen I–V* of the *Schwarze Hefte*, from the period 1942 to 1948) was published only after the appearance of my book. There I cited a passage that had been made public by Donatella di Cesare, but I had not yet read the volume. One passage in particular drew my attention and seemed to me to demand the following supplement.

1

In the *Anmerkungen I* of volume 97, the notebook pages 138 and 139 (on pages 90–91 of the volume) present a group of three paragraphs whose theme offers a character that is, if not unique, at least accentuated here in an exceptional way. (I do not claim to have mastered the entire contents of the *Schwarze Hefte*, but it seems to me that this theme does not receive elsewhere the same striking form.) It can be summarized very simply: Christianity should have been capable of resisting the decline of the West.

Before entering into this passage, I will give a few indications oriented by this thought as it appears in the preceding volumes of the *Notebooks* (I will refrain from exploring it more broadly, in the *Beiträge* in particular, which would require a separate study).

One can point to several passages, within the continuity of a motif that I have already indicated, in which Heidegger insists on a profound difference between one aspect of Christianity and another. Very often the ecclesiastical and apologetic elements are distinguished from a supposedly true faith, as well as from theology, "Hegelian metaphysics," or the thought of Kierkegaard. Thus in volume 94 (page 388), it is a question of an increasing exhaustion of Christian faith, which presumes a former vitality. One also finds this (pages 522–23): "Christianity awakened and fashioned the forces of spirit, of discipline and firmness of soul which must not be separated from Western history, all the less so in that they are still active, albeit in a deviated manner, and in that they still give to some individuals a 'hold.' But it is not there that the great decisions take place. Christianity long ago lost all power of originarity; it rendered its own history [*Geschichte*] merely historical [*historisch*]."[1] A comparable assertion is also found in volume 96 (on pages 261–62).

There is therefore (pending a more complete overview) a recurrent indication of the internal difference between, on the one hand, a certain initial dynamic of Christianity and, on the other, its intensification both in the religion of salvation and in a collusion with metaphysics and the culture of the West. Christianity is thus said to have lost its proper vigor. It must therefore have first possessed it. It is this possession of a distinct properness, now disappeared "since long ago," that is marked with a rare force in the passage from volume 97 that I would like to read. (Just how long ago this loss reached its completion—including when its effects are still felt—, this is not said. Everything permits us to suspect that it is in a way an originary loss. We would perhaps not be too far from Nietzsche's "there was only one Christian" and therefore from a theme of initial purity annulled in its very surging forth, which could offer an analogy with "the forgetting of being.")

This properness is enunciated here in the word *Eindeutigkeit*: univocality. The last sentence of the passage states the following (aimed at Jaspers, who is named in the previous sentence): "One cites passages from Paul's letters as fundamental truths and thus leaves out everything that could demand the univocality of what is Christian" (*des Christlichen*, that is, of the Christian element rather than of Christianity as *Christentum* or Christendom).

This univocality gives the final word at the end of a passage that began with a reproach addressed to Christianity for never having done anything to counter the "thronging rush, the frenzy and equivocality [*Zweideutigkeit*, ambiguity] of the will to will" and for having, on the contrary, "everywhere supported exhaustion [*Ohnmacht*]." The will to will (or "for" will—*der Wille* zum *Wille*) is one of the ways to designate the metaphysical closure par excellence: the complete deviation of all correspondence to *beyng*. In willing itself for itself, the will wills beings and wills itself as a being. It is not possible here to enter any further into an analysis of this motif. I would only like to point out that in the same volume Heidegger writes, "Will is obstruction. All that obstructs (*das Sperrige*) comes from will." Meaning: all that obstructs the opening toward *beyng*.

The equivocality of this will responds to the equivocality that characterizes metaphysics—that is, the maintenance of an equivocation between being and beings, and consequently their confusion or the substitution of the second for the first. In a word: the meaning of being is univocal (whether one takes the genitive as subjective or objective). (Which does not mean that there is not another univocality, that of technics, and this is mentioned several times in the *Notebooks*.)

Heidegger specifies then that even when a will that might seem opposed to the will to will has been able to manifest, Christianity "as such" has not conquered but has only calculated a pact in order to participate in the movement that leads to a deviation of "the discord of beyng" toward "the discord within the will to will"—that is, that leads to the world war between the pretenders to the domination of their own will. Clearly stated (and passing over here the numerous analyses and references within the *Notebooks*), the confrontation between metaphysical, racial, dominating, and calculating wills—namely, the Nazis and the Jews, but also Jewish Americans or democrats, or Jewish Bolsheviks—engulfs the opening of being, the tension it spans between its meaning and the beings whose meaning it gives, in "what is most extreme of the public and vulgar character of humanity." In that regard, one can at the same time treat this confrontation as "world peace."

2

Christianity appears thus insofar as it conforms to a *historisch* historicity, for it "objectifies historiality as a calculation of something 'eternal' which in truth is 'revealed' and 'is' only in the unicity [or uniqueness] of a destining [*eines Geschickes*] and for which it 'has' 'its' time, which it itself appropriates [*ereignet*] and brings with it—but from which its unique one is removed if it is ordered by the historical frame of a temporal sequence."

This sentence is very remarkable: in it Heidegger mobilizes Christian terms—"eternal," "reveal"—as well as the major motif of the "proper time" and the "unique" or "only" one. It must be said that "proper time" as it is outlined here corresponds rather well to messianic time as the time that the Messiah decides of himself and for himself. To his disciples who ask when he will return to restore the Kingdom, Christ replies that it is not for them to know the "times and seasons—*chronous hè kairous*" (Acts 1:7; the expression is also found in Paul). Among many others, this reference cannot simply be absent from the text that we are reading here.

This text pursues immediately, in a new paragraph, by declaring, "The fear of the historial, that is, of the unicity of destiny, the inability-to-let-come the appropriative event in the once-ness of the unique one, belongs to the essence of history [*Historie*]." The "once-ness of the unique one" awkwardly translates *die Einstigkeit des Einzigen* (which must also have pleased Heidegger in its assonance). The adverb *einst* has the sense of "once long ago" (or sometimes also in the distant future). It comes from *ein* (one) and can be compared to the "once" of "once upon a time." It is a question therefore of a unique occurrence, immemorial and also to come, of the Unique itself. In the essay of 1938–40 on *The History of Beyng* (volume 69 of the GA), Heidegger writes that "beyng is the what-takes-place-once [*das Einstige*]," and he emphasizes the double value of past and future in the term.

The refusal of the "once" of the unique—or of being as event—characterizes the falsification of the historial destining into a historicity "deprived of destining"—of destination, of aptness to correspond to the event. Heidegger devotes a dozen lines to a harsh attack on history, psychology, and philosophy for their "thoughtlessness," which ends up "coupling with Christianity and faith" to the point of degrading itself in a "moralism" of which Jaspers is named as the representative, having become incapable of recognizing his own betrayal. It is thus a reference to him in the last sentence: "One cites passages from Paul's letters as fundamental truths and one thus leaves aside everything that might favor the univocality of what is Christian."

3

There is therefore a Christian univocality that should have manifested itself and that would have countered the metaphysical equivocality. Univocality—that is to say, also clarity, self-evidence. In sum, a Christian self-evidence and certainty, capable of rising to the level of a thought of the unicity of being, were lost by Christianity itself. This loss is at once the effect of a sort of historical perversion, through a calculation of the possibility of domination, and yet also as though introduced from the start: it is not clear whether Paul is considered in himself or above all insofar as he was put to use by "moralism."

These considerations open some complex prospects of exploration concerning Heidegger's relation to Christianity. What at first appears as a slight suspicion, based on the signals noted earlier, gives rise in this passage to a declaration: Christianity failed at something that should have fallen to it. That it failed from the outset does not mean that it always lacked a proper destination for "univocality."

This is not the place to advance further in this direction. But it is the place where we must ask how this relation to Christianity is or is not connected to anti-Semitism. Earlier in these same *Anmerkungen I*, the relation of Christianity to Judaism is touched upon. On page 20 Heidegger posits a principle of genealogy based on the axiom that "every anti- must arise from the same essential ground as that against which it is anti- ." So it is with the Antichrist or anti-Christianity: it is still in some way Christian. In the earlier *Notebooks* it happened that Nazi anti-Christianity, particularly in the form of an "affirmation of life," is treated with derision. Here it serves rather to go further back in the genealogy: Christianity, we are immediately reminded, issued from Judaism. From this it is concluded that the former participates in the latter. The latter is immediately characterized as "the principle of destruction in the epoch of the Christian West, that is, of metaphysics." The destruction is then imputed above all to Marx and to the determination by "the economy, that is, organisation—that is, the biological—that is, the 'people'": one slips very quickly from communism to Nazism.

The next paragraph continues by evoking the struggle of "what is Jewish [nominalized adjective: *das Jüdische*] in the metaphysical sense, against what is Jewish." This struggle— at once Jewish/Nazi and Bolshevik/American—determines "the high point of self-annihilation in history." This motif has already appeared in the earlier *Notebooks*; here it is linked to the Christian and/or anti-Christian motif in a way that does not allow one to suspect the slightest protest against any loss of Christian "univocality." Without it being specified, one is meant to understand that Christianity has made a pact with destruction. Christian anti-Judaism or anti-Semitism receives no attention.

However, the following paragraph recalls the thought of the Greek "first beginning" that "remained outside of Judaism, that is, of Christianity." Then in the next paragraph a single line adds, "The darkening of a world never reaches the silent light of being [*Sein*]."

4

Because Christianity is Jewish, it has nothing to do with the destining of being. It harbored, however, a univocality that could have raised it to the level of an opposition to the destruction, Jewish in its principle, of this destining. Christianity is therefore Jewish and non-Jewish. But well before Heidegger Christianity contorted itself into this kind of double bind. It attempted to take on and to surpass its provenance as much as it attempted to disavow and reject it. Paul is the major witness to this double process. It is he who declares that henceforth there is neither Jew nor Greek. Christianity must have a complete originarity, but this originarity is constituted on the basis of a Jewish provenance. What Paul carries away in an assumption that one could call Roman, Heidegger for his part refuses, in the name of an originary Greek light, intact in its primordial destining.

However, he cannot refrain from indicating something like the possibility of another destining, no less luminous perhaps, that would have stifled itself as Christianity, but that could have or should have taken place.

This question, too, cannot be treated here. However, it must be emphasized to what extent anti-Semitism thus finds itself placed on its most authentic foundation, which is Christian (and singularly Pauline). Christianity defined itself by the rejection of its provenance—or, more broadly, perhaps we must say that monotheism (the refusal of gods considered as idols) determined itself as a sort of regime of foundation, of sacred autochthony, and that it thus engaged itself in an interminable process of provenance, of genealogy (both backward and forward), or even of the errancy and wandering with which it itself attempted to break by inventing itself as auto-engenderment.

However that may be, it was necessary for it to reject its provenance. Within the phenomenon of the birth of the premodern world there is a rejection internal to this world, as if it had to conjure away its own uncertainty regarding its legitimacy. The Jew is quickly charged with the crime and must bear it from anti-Judaism to modern anti-Semitism, covered with the most miserable rags of an accusation of essence: the Jew is calculation, machination, the will to domination, the principle of destruction, since he was not able or willing to recognize the new origin. It is in this that Heidegger's anti-Semitism is banal: it carts around the vulgarity spread by an incessant discourse crystalized as hateful, racist denunciation, at a time when the Christian and post-Christian world itself has begun to tear itself apart.

Heidegger sees the disaster of this world. He interprets it simultaneously as a Greek and as a Christian; he wants to be above the fray and to endure a forgetting that being itself could bring to an end by "returning," as he writes in 1946 in "The Anaximander Fragment." But as a Christian—since he is one, despite everything; he even is one in the most banal way, steeped as he is in theology and spirituality—he finds it necessary to disqualify the people who have not recognized Christ. But if Christ bore the possibility of another destining, did the latter have anything to do with the Jewish provenance? And if not, could Christ somehow have been a little bit Greek? This absurdity may have tormented Heidegger. But not too much, for anti-Semitism conveniently offered him suitable material for explaining the Western catastrophe. Which assumes, first, that the perception of a catastrophe is the only one possible—once again, a question of univocality—and then that one accept more or less secretly, in some private notebooks, reducing metaphysics to the biologizing racism of those same Nazis who are reproached for the misery of their thoughtlessness.

Heidegger, we know all too well, made no effort to reconsider the question of anti-Semitism. However, he did get a little worried that his anti-Christianity might be misunderstood. In the *Anmerkungen II* he specifies (page 199 of the volume) that he should not be taken still for a Christian (which, however, would be coherent with his genealogical principle!). He specifies that he "cannot" be Christian and that this impossibility has to do with the fact that, "in Christian terms, I do not have grace. I will never have it as long as thought remains a demand for my path." There would therefore be a deep incompatibility between grace and thought. One cannot help remarking, however, that "having grace" is precisely not a very rigorous Christian expression, if grace belongs only to God who gives it. Let us say that this is at the least a thought that remains quite cursory. Likewise one can point out that it occurs in a passage that challenges the "demythologisation of Christianity" on the grounds that it remains within theological Christianity. Perhaps he could have shown a slightly sharper attention . . . (to be sure, he is trying to be careful in his treatment of Bultmann, but then why?).

Later (*Anmerkungen IV*, page 409) Heidegger shows himself to be even more simplistic when he writes that "perhaps the god of the philosophers would after all be more divine than the God of Abraham, who can tolerate no other god beside him and whose son Jesus sent all those who didn't love him to roast in hell." A Voltairian banality this time . . . Heidegger as a man of the Enlightenment?

One finds in him an embarrassment before or with Christianity. Perhaps he is at bottom traversed by this archeophilic movement, whose insistence throughout Christianity is remarkable. From Nietzsche to Kierkegaard and to Dietrich Bonhoeffer, as well as many others, there is an insistent self-deconstruction of Christianity that shows itself to be haunted by a sort of promise that goes against the grain, so to speak: a promise to take Christianity out of itself, without for all that leading it back to Judaism—rather by going further (and more deeply) back *and* by going beyond both (and beyond Islam, one could add). It is possible that Heidegger may have confusedly shared such a concern. Not enough, however, not to have held firm to a Greek origin too purely dazzling to be sharable, and consequently to a sordid anti-Semitism and an enmired anti-Christianism.

In the same volume (page 453) one finds the affirmation that it is essential "that in thinking we take on as our own [as proper] the lack of the divinity (the reserve), in that there is a lack to appropriate in appropriation." If this difficult (uselessly convoluted?) sentence means that the resource of the divine must always be lacking in order to leave open our exposure to being—then it is at least possible to affirm that it was not at all necessary to pass by way of this vulgarity, this indignity, and this sinking into the mire. On the contrary.

But perhaps thereby, and despite himself, Heidegger will have made us more sensitive to what is covered over not by forgetting, but by the unforgettable of anti-Semitism: a fracture and a closing-off, conjoined, of the West.

The sentence I just quoted might resonate in a surprising continuity with the one written by Jean-François almost thirty years ago in the last sentence of *Heidegger and "the jews,"* evoking Celan and thinking perhaps of his "Praised be you, Nobody": " 'Celan' is neither the beginning nor the end of Heidegger; he is his lack: what is missing in him, what he misses, and whose lack he is lacking."

Jean-Luc Nancy, March 2016

Acknowledgments

A first version of this study was presented at the colloquium organized in Wuppertal by the Martin Heidegger Institut, October 30 and November 1, 2014, entitled "Heidegger und die Juden" [Heidegger and the Jews]. It was published, in German, in Peter Trawny and Andrew J. Mitchell, eds., *Heidegger, die Juden, noch einmal* (Frankfurt am Main: Vittorio Klostermann, 2015).

The translator would like to thank Jean-Luc Nancy for his generous and helpful responses to multiple queries during the preparation of this translation.

Notes

Translator's Preface. Both/And: Heidegger's Equivocality

1. At the moment when Nancy wrote this text, there were no translations of the *Schwarze Hefte* into French or English. Since then, an English translation has begun to appear. The first volume (*Gesamtausgabe* 94) has been published as *Ponderings II–VI: Black Notebooks 1931–1938*, trans. Richard Rojcewicz (Bloomington: Indiana University Press, 2016). There will be two more volumes of *Ponderings*, in addition to numerous further *Black Notebooks* under various titles, including the *Anmerkungen* (Remarks) discussed by Nancy in the Supplement. Nancy tends to refer to the *Ponderings* using the German title, *Überlegungen*, and in this translation I have kept these references as such (since they reflect the text he is quoting/translating); but he sometimes refers to them in French as "Réflexions" (Reflections). I have chosen to maintain a literal translation for these references; the reader should keep in mind that they refer to the texts translated into English as *Ponderings*.

2. For similar reasons, I have not sought to align my translations of Nancy's translations with the newly available first
volume of the *Ponderings*. Readers who wish to compare will be
able to find the passages in question by referring to the German
Gesamtausgabe pagination referred to by Nancy, which is also
provided as running heads on each page of the *Ponderings*.
Likewise the page numbers of the original notebooks themselves, which Nancy refers to in his Supplement, are also
supplied in the margins of the *Ponderings*.

3. "Et alors? et alors?" This was his emphatic rhetorical
question regarding the issue of relative proportions, as given
in the first spoken presentation of this material at the 2014
conference in Wuppertal referred to in the book's liminal note.
(As of August 2016, the audio of this presentation in French was
available on YouTube, labeled, "'Banalité de Heidegger,'
Jean-Luc Nancy, 2014"; see https://www.youtube.com/watch?v
=c8zxB9NKIOU.)

4. Is it necessary nonetheless to stress yet further that
Nancy's invocation of "banality" in no way implies a lessening
of the charges, or of the weight of condemnation, directed
against Heidegger? As part of an exchange of emails regarding
my queries for this translation, Nancy expressed a concern
(based on some responses to his arguments in France, Italy, and
elsewhere) that such a misinterpretation might persist despite
everything. Despite, for example, Nancy's own very clear and
emphatic statement, in italics, that what is important now is not
only condemnation, but above all analysis, not in order to
mitigate the former, but on the contrary for the sake of "*thinking
the deep reasons for our condemnations.*" It is precisely this task
that takes the questions at hand beyond the relatively circumscribed, if at times passionate, debates regarding Heidegger
himself, and certainly beyond any rancorous or apologetic
fixation on this figure.

5. One might notice the irony, and apparent inappropriate-
ness, of referring to Heidegger's thought as a "resource" (a word
I take from Nancy, used in reference to Heidegger's radical and
essential desubstantializing of being and of the language in

which it is designated). It is obviously not meant in the sense of a "standing reserve" that could be extracted, exploited, etc., but rather as a matter for thinking—and no doubt even for forms of critique that Heidegger himself was unable to formulate.

1

All notes are the author's except where otherwise indicated and when reference is made to English translations.

1. The *Notebooks* from the years 1931–41 have been edited by Peter Trawny and published under the general title *Überlegungen* ("Reflections"), subtitled *Schwarze Hefte* ("Black Notebooks"), followed by the numbers assigned to the notebooks, making up volumes 94–96 of Heidegger's *Gesamtausgabe* (Frankfurt am Main: Vittorio Klostermann, 2014) (translation of quotations are my own). The subsequent years are in preparation: there are thirty-four *Black Notebooks* in all, covering the period from 1931 to around 1969. [The *Gesamtausgabe* of Heidegger's works will henceforth be cited as GA, followed by the volume and page numbers. An English translation of the *Black Notebooks* is in preparation. The first volume (GA 94) has recently appeared as *Ponderings II–VI: Black Notebooks 1931–1938*, trans. Richard Rojcewicz (Bloomington: Indiana University Press, 2016). As in the present note, Nancy occasionally refers to these texts with the French word "Réflexions," which I have rendered literally throughout.—Trans.]

2. I here leave to one side what is directly connected to the state of Israel, which did not exist during the period under consideration.

3. Danièle Lochak, "Ecrire, se taire . . . Réflexions sur la doctrine antisémite de Vichy," in *Le Genre Humain, Le droit antisémite de Vichy*, nos. 30–31 (May 1996). (To understand the title of this article, it is necessary to specify that "doctrine" in the technical juridical sense designates in France all of the commentaries produced by academic jurists. The Germans sometimes say "*die Rechtsdoktrin*" but more often "*die Rechtslehre*" or "*die jurisitsche Lehre*.") [The English term is *jurisprudence*.—Trans.]

4. See, for example, Heidegger, *Überlegungen V*, GA 94, 370. I take the opportunity of this first reference to pay homage to the work of Peter Trawny, editor and commentator of volumes 94 to 96. This does not mean that I entirely agree with all of his commentaries, but I salute their precision, determination, and courage. I take the opportunity also to point out that Maurice Olender refers at length to Trawny in the preface to the Italian edition of his book *Razza e destino* (Milan: Bompiani, 2014); translation of *Race sans histoire* (Paris: Seuil, 2009), in which it is a question of Heidegger, among others.

5. Ibid., 411.

2

1. [Nancy is here (and in the last sentence of the previous section) playing on a grammatical distinction that cannot be transposed into English, whereby "being" in its ontological sense can be expressed, in both French and German, either with or without an article (*das Sein/Sein, l'être/être*), a distinction that is significant for Heidegger's thought. Matters are confused in English in that the expression "the being" is used to translate not "das Sein" but "der Seiende," the ontical term for *beings*—and so the very thing from which Heidegger means to differentiate "being" as *Sein.*—Trans.]

2. Jacques Derrida, *La voix et le phénomène* (Paris: PUF, 1967), 27; English: *Speech and Phenomena*, trans. David B. Allison (Evanston: Northwestern University Press, 1973), 25. If I indicate at this point Derrida's reprise of the motif of "arriving," of history (therefore), and of a (re)beginning of or in the history of being or of/in being as history, this is in order to indicate already—before returning to it later—the initial point of a dehiscence opened in relation to Heidegger's thought itself and as a way to diverge from it in a discernible and continuous manner.

3. Martin Heidegger, *Überlegungen IV*, GA 94, 241.

4. See Heidegger, *Überlegungen VII*, GA 95, 63.

5. Contained in Heidegger, GA 95 and 96.

6. Incessantly repeated in these notes, as it is in the *Beiträge*, the word *Machenschaft* can correspond to something like "scheming [*manigance*]" or "maneuvers [*menées*]" (like this term, it is today most often used in the plural), but it evokes first for Heidegger the general enterprise of modern "making" (*machen*) as production, as opposed to "doing" (*tun*) as action, or even "creation" or "giving birth [*mise au monde*]." Technics is therefore implicated in it, and thereby also the domination of the object: the *Beiträge* offer the word "*das Gegenständlich-Machenschaftliche*"—that is, something like "the objectal-machinated" by which (it is said) modern man is so blinded that beings have withdrawn from him "as have all the more beyng and its truth"; see Heidegger, *Beiträge zur Philosophie* (1936–38), GA 65 (Frankfurt am Main: Vittorio Klostermann, 2003), 111; English: *Contributions to Philosophy (Of the Event)*, trans. Richard Rojcewicz and Daniella Vallega-Neu (Bloomington: Indiana University Press, 2012), 88 [translation modified to reflect Nancy's text].

7. See Heidegger, *Überlegungen XV*, GA 96, 261.

8. Ibid., 264.

9. This corresponds to the end of volume 96. The volumes of the years that follow have yet to appear, but it seems unlikely that they would reverse the general tendency of Heidegger's thinking. This is already verified in some of the later fragments that have been quoted (see the note in Section 11 of this volume referring to Donatella di Cesare).

10. Heidegger, *La pauvreté (die Armut)*, translated into French and published in 2004 by Philippe Lacoue-Labarthe (Strasbourg: Presses Universitaires de Strasbourg).

11. See Heidegger, *Überlegungen XV*, GA 96, 276.

12. See Heidegger, *Überlegungen XII*, GA 96, 48.

13. A laborious translation of a ponderous text: "Nicht 'durch' diesen als seinen 'Schöpfer,' sondern zu ihm entschieden in der / Entgegnung des Wesens von Gottschaft und Menschentum wird aus dem Menschenwesen ein Volk, das die Gründerschaft des Wesens der Wahrheit er-trägt" (ibid.).

3

1. "Die Frage nach der Rolle des *Weltjudentums* ist keine rassische, sondern die metaphysische Frage nach der Art von Menschentümlichkeit, die *schlechthin ungebunden* die Entwurzelung alles Seienden aus dem Sein als weltgeschichtliche 'Aufgabe' übernehmen kann" (Heidegger, *Überlegungen XIV*, in GA 96, 243) [Heidegger's emphasis]. With the help of Clemens Härle I believe it is possible to specify the following: the word *Menschentümlichkeit* seems to be a creation of Heidegger's and is indeed perhaps a *hapax*. It attempts to designate a possible modality of being-human. In a sense, the expression "*die Art von Menschentümlichkeit*" would signify "the specific kind [*espèce*] of modality, or of manner, of being-human." I choose "type" to translate *Art* (a very common word that Heidegger uses frequently)—rather than "kind" (*espèce* or *genre*), or "sort"—so as to have a term that is, on the one hand, sufficiently marked and, on the other, without connotations that are too biological. I am thus doing justice to Heidegger's stated claim, and if the word "type" produces an allusion to the anti-Semitic lexicon, I did not seek this. However, I gladly take the opportunity to refer to all of Philippe Lacoue-Labarthe's reflections on the "typology" proper to "metaphysics" in the critical sense of the word.

2. Lacoue-Labarthe, *La fiction du politique* (Paris: Bourgois, 1987), 75–76; English: *Heidegger, Art and Politics: The Fiction of the Political*, trans. Chris Turner (Oxford and Cambridge, Mass.: Basil Blackwell, 1990), 48–49.

3. "Rassenkunde, Vorgeschichtskunde und Volkskunde machen die 'wissenschaftliche' Grundlegung der völkisch-politischen Weltanschauungen aus" (Heidegger, *Überlegungen XI*, in GA 95, 429).

4

1. Heidegger, *Überlegungen VII*, GA 95, 56.

2. Heidegger, *Überlegungen XII*, GA 96, 38 [Nancy's interpolations].

3. Ibid., 32.

4. [The word I have rendered here as "ending" is *achèvement*, which denotes ending as completion and fulfillment but can also imply ending as termination, finishing, finishing off, connotations that are all in play here. The word occurs again in the next two sentences, along with the related verb "*s'achever*."—Trans.]

5

1. Martin Heidegger, *Vorträge und Aufsätze* (Pfullingen: Neske, 1954), 69. For an English translation, see "Overcoming Metaphysics," in *The End of Philosophy*, trans. Joan Stambaugh (New York: Harper and Row, 1973).

2. Thus I translate—to avoid more colloquial terms such as "*combine* [ploy]" or "*embrouille* [muddle, swindle]," whose connotations are nonetheless related—the word "*durcheinander-mischen* [mixing up]." One could also render it with "scheming." These special aptitudes attributed to the Jews are the very characteristics of the *Machenschaft* in which the devastation is accomplished. The passage in question is found in Heidegger, *Überlegungen VIII*, GA 95, 97.

3. "*Das Riesige*" is for Heidegger a characteristic trait of the West in decline. The "Reflections" return often to this point.

4. Heidegger, *Überlegungen VIII*, GA 95, 97.

5. Immanuel Kant, "General Remark: On Religious Sects," in the Appendix to Part 1 of *The Conflict of the Faculties*, trans. Mary J. Gregor (Lincoln: University of Nebraska Press, 1979), 95. The context as a whole shows clearly that for Kant it is a question of the disappearance of dogmatic and ritual Judaism and of all religious "sectarianism" for the benefit of "one shepherd and one flock." The "conversion of the Jews," a very old Christian motif evoked in the same passage, clearly evokes the conjunction between a rejection of Judaism and a desire to find (again) a religious unity beyond the differences between religions. The Christian (and/or the rational, philosophical, etc.) relation to Judaism did not cease to oscillate between condemnation and

conversion, between the affirmation of a deep irreconcilability and that of a necessary reconciliation.

6. One can imagine that in the *Selbstvernichtung* evoked previously, the annihilation of the Jews would represent the central moment and therefore the auto-exclusion of the *Bodenlos*. However, this hypothesis does not square well with the mutual destruction of the two sides of the West (communist and capitalist) since the Jews are themselves placed on both sides— unless one considers that they themselves destroy themselves in the confrontation. But Heidegger—whatever he may have known or thought of the camps at the time of these "reflections"— cannot be ignorant of the Nazi treatment of the Jews, including *Kristallnacht* and the Nuremberg laws, which had nothing to do with any self-destruction. Would it then be necessary to go so far as to think of the Russian pogroms as the other side of the "self-destruction"? This would be as grotesque as it is hideous. But then why is one led into this kind of speculation, if not because Heidegger never said a single word on any aspect of the anti-Semitic persecutions, which nonetheless would have deserved the same overt disdain and hostility he directed at "biological" anti-Semitism (see section 11 in this volume)?

7. Heidegger, *Überlegungen VIII*, GA 95, 133 [Nancy's interpolation].

6

1. Heidegger, *Überlegungen VIII*, GA 95, 340. (This passage goes on to emphasize that this determination is foreign to every idea of race or of "*Volkstum*.")

2. Heidegger writes literally "*Mischmasch*"; *Überlegungen X*, GA 95, 324.

3. Heidegger, "Letter on Humanism" (1946), trans. Frank A. Capuzzi, in *Pathmarks*, ed. William McNeill (Cambridge: Cambridge University Press, 1998), 263.

4. Peter Trawny has devoted a book to this question: *Heidegger and the Myth of a Jewish World Conspiracy*, trans. Andrew J. Mitchell (Chicago: University of Chicago Press, 2015).

5. We will return to this: at each stage, anti-Semitism was the product of a discontent, a malaise, or an ill-being, and of a detestation and a fear *of self* within the Christian West, its power, its humanism. . . .

6. One can refer to the many occurrences of the word *grob* (crude, coarse, rude) in the text of the *Überlegungen*.

7. For example in Heidegger, *Überlegungen VIII*, GA 95, 132.

8. Ibid., 99 [Nancy's interpolation].

9. "*Zerstörung*" is a word often repeated in the *Notebooks*, most often to designate the devastating work accomplished by Western scheming.

7

1. According to Otto Weininger, in a document found in the Theodor Lessing archives. See Martine-Sophie Benoit, "Theodor Lessing et le concept de 'haine de soi juive,'" in *La haine de soi: Difficiles identités* (Brussels: Complexe, 2000).

2. Heidegger, *Überlegungen VI*, GA 94, 465–66. [Nancy's interpolations.]

3. On the question of whether or not the extermination of the Jews of Europe had a sacrificial character, as well as on the role of sacrifice in Heidegger and/or in the philosophical tradition, much has been written and debated—notably by Lyotard, Derrida, and Lacoue-Labarthe, but also by other authors of several countries. This would be the object of a specific study.

4. On the theme of erring and/or wandering—of *Irre* as a "long erring" that must be risked (see Heidegger, *Überlegungen VI*, GA 94, 508, for example) or as "wandering in a dreamland" (ibid., 152) (among a hundred possible examples of the double meaning of this term), it would be necessary to return to this elsewhere and to look closely at Peter Trawny's book on this question; Trawny, *The Freedom to Fail: Heidegger's Anarchy*, trans. Ian Alexander Moore and Christopher Turner (Cambridge: Polity, 2015).

5. See Paul's Letter to the Ephesians, 4:20–24.

6. In the sense that it has become entirely "breeding," according to a term from Nietzsche quoted in Heidegger, *Überlegungen XIV*, GA 96, 189.

7. See Heidegger, *Überlegungen XIII*, GA 96, 111.

8

1. See Daniel Boyarin, *Border Lines: The Partition of Judaeo-Christianity* (Philadelphia: University of Pennsylvania Press, 2004).

2. As a first approach I can only refer here to the course given in 1964 by Jacques Derrida, *Heidegger: La question de l'Être et l'Histoire; Cours d l'ENS-Ulm (1964–1965)* (Paris: Galilée, 2014); English: *Heidegger: The Question of Being and History*, trans. Geoffrey Bennington (Chicago: University of Chicago Press, 2016).

3. Nothing, no self, since that is when the "self" came about. Michel Foucault's analyses of the "care of the self" (*The History of Sexuality*, vol. 3, *The Care of the Self*, trans. Robert Hurley [New York: Vintage, 1986]) are eloquent in this regard. If one wants to go back before Christianity and Latinity, it is no doubt necessary to interrogate that which in "monotheism" gives rise to the emergence of a "self" (interpellated, called, judged, loved, summoned . . .).

4. See the study by Pierre Gisel in *L'Antijudaïsme en philosophie et en théologie*, ed. Antoine Guggenheim and Danielle Cohen-Levinas (Paris: Parole et silence, 2014).

5. I outlined this thesis in Jean-Luc Nancy, *Adoration: The Deconstruction of Christianity II*, trans. John McKeane (New York: Fordham University Press, 2013).

6. See Philippe Lacoue-Labarthe's reflections in *La réponse d'Ulysse et autres textes sur l'Occident* (Paris: Lignes, 2013).

7. Martin Heidegger, *Überlegungen X*, GA 95, 294. This critique also corresponds to the often-repeated critique of "salvation," a notion that is assimilated to "calculation."

8. Heidegger, *Überlegungen VI*, GA 94, 476.

9. Ibid., 475.

10. There emerges here, of course, the possibility of a secret affinity, conscious or not, between Heidegger, a certain Judaism,

and a certain Christianity. After the work of Marlène Zarader and a few others, and after the work of Jean-François Lyotard as well, a space is open for further work on what the latter called "the thought of the Other arranged into thought of Being" (Lyotard, *Heidegger et "les juifs"* [Paris: Galilée, 1988], 47; English: *Heidegger and "the jews,"* trans. Andreas Michel and Mark Roberts [Minneapolis: University of Minnesota Press, 1990], 23). It has only barely been opened. . . .

11. Heidegger, *Überlegungen VII*, GA 95, 34.

9

1. Jean-François Lyotard spoke of this already in *Heidegger and "the jews."*

2. See Maurice Olender, *Race sans histoire* (Paris: Seuil, 2009).

3. I do not mean to imply that there would no longer be any need to reflect on the historicity—the processuality, the becoming—of the West. On the contrary. It is difficult to deny the linkages that go from Athens and Rome to Paris, London, Berlin, Moscow, Auschwitz, Hiroshima, and elsewhere. But it is in no way inevitable that we consider this as an organic and oriented development.—We are far from beginning to think through this question, like all those raised by Heidegger's anti-Semitism—that is, the self-hatred embodied in the most vehement will to affirmation of self.

4. I am referring to the often-quoted phrase on the camps and the gas chambers from the original lecture ("Das Ge-Stell") on which the essay "The Question Concerning Technology" is based, and to a statement on "the horror of the gas chambers" in the passage cited in a note in section 11 of this volume. For the former, see Martin Heidegger, *Bremer und Freiburger Vorträge*, GA 79, 27; English: "Positionality," in *Bremen and Freiburg Lectures*, trans. Andrew J. Mitchell (Indianapolis: Indiana University Press, 2014), 27.

5. Heidegger, *Überlegungen XV*, GA 96, 251.

6. To be more specific: the law of the initial as a "self" of the initial that itself institutes itself in every sense: that inaugurates

itself, creates itself, and initiates itself into its own proper mystery.

7. Heidegger, *Überlegungen XI*, GA 95, 430.

8. Elisabeth Rigal, "De l'histoire comme destinerrance" (unpublished text presented at the conference "Héritage et survivances de Jacques Derrida," Paris, November 2014).

9. Heidegger, *Überlegungen XI*, GA 95, 410.

10

1. Martin Heidegger, *Überlegungen XI*, GA 95, 422.

2. Heidegger, *Überlegungen XIV*, GA 96, 225.

3. Ibid., 116.

4. Ibid. [Nancy's interpolations.]

5. We must obviously recall here that Lyotard's *Heidegger and "the jews,"* mentioned previously, remains the great precursor in this affair. To which must be added, in relation to another aspect of the inquiry, Marlène Zarader's *La dette impensée: Heidegger et l'héritage hébraïque* (Paris: Seuil, 1990); English: *The Unthought Debt: Heidegger and the Hebraic Heritage*, trans. Bettina Bergo (Stanford: Stanford University Press, 2006).

6. Heidegger, *Überlegungen XV*, GA 96, 273.

7. Genesis 6:8.

11

1. Martin Heidegger, *Überlegungen XV*, GA 96, 251. [Nancy's interpolation.]

2. On this date, as was the case in most German cities, Jewish businesses of Freiburg im Breisgau were attacked and the synagogue was burned. Around one hundred Jews of the city were deported a few months later (many others had left the city beginning in 1933, including some students and teachers who had been excluded from the university).

3. See the excerpt from a *Notebook* of 1945 quoted by Donatella di Cesare in her interview in *Hohe Luft* of 10 February 2015. In this excerpt, however, Heidegger distinguishes the current state of Germany and "the horror of the gas chambers."

4. Jacques Derrida, *Of Spirit: Heidegger and the Question*, trans. Geoffrey Bennington and Rachel Bowlby (Chicago: University of Chicago Press, 1989), chap. 8, 74.

5. Heidegger, *Überlegungen III*, GA 94, 173. [Heidegger's emphasis; Nancy's interpolation.]

6. Ibid., 189.

7. Collected in Heidegger's GA 69 (*Die Geschichte des Seyns*). English: *The History of Beyng*, trans. Jeffrey Powell and William McNeill (Bloomington: Indiana University Press, 2015). These texts were not published during the author's lifetime but were conceived as possible public lectures and are therefore distinct from the notes in the *Notebooks*.

8. GA 69, 213: "*erstanfängliche Verborgenheit.*" In what follows I gloss several passages from the same volume without multiplying the references.

9. And no doubt it emerges once again, in a different way, in the late text "Time and Being" (from 1962), in *On Time and Being*, trans. Joan Stambaugh (New York: Harper and Row, 1972), 1–24: here one would have to consider Heidegger's entire itinerary—assuming one still had any appetite for this. . . .

12

1. Martin Heidegger, *Überlegungen XII*, GA 96, 22.

2. One can find very legible traces of this in Heidegger's course from 1920 to 1921 (GA 60), entitled *The Phenomenology of Religious Life*, trans. Matthias Fritsch and Jennifer Anna Gosetti-Ferencei (Bloomington: Indiana University Press, 2010), but this is not the place to show this. On the close relations that Heidegger establishes at that time between "religious life" and historicity, one can consult Sylvain Camilleri, *Phénoménologie de la religion et herméneutique théologique dans la pensée du jeune Heidegger* (Dordrecht: Springer, 2008). One also finds there some very precise observations on Heidegger's relation, during that period, to Judaism and Judeo-Christianity.

3. See the final paragraphs of Karl Marx, "On the Jewish Question."

4. Joseph Conrad, at the end of his "Author's Note" to *Under Western Eyes*. It is well known that this text, in which Conrad evokes a "banality" of evil, is quite likely (along with other sources) to have inspired Hannah Arendt.

5. Heidegger, *Überlegungen III*, GA 94, 128.

Coda

1. Martin Heidegger, *Überlegungen XIII*, GA 96, 157.

Supplement

1. [Nancy's interpolations.]